W9-BCT-717

MARY

VIRGIN, MOTHER, AND QUEEN

A BIBLE STUDY GUIDE FOR CATHOLICS

FR. MITCH PACWA, S.J.

Our Sunday Visitor Publishing Division
Our Sunday Visitor, Inc.
Huntington, IN 46750

Nihil Obstat
Msgr. Michael Heintz, Ph.D.
Censor Librorum

Imprimatur
✠ Kevin C. Rhoades
Bishop of Fort Wayne-South Bend
November 22, 2013

The *Nihil Obstat* and *Imprimatur* are official declarations that a book is free from doctrinal or moral error. It is not implied that those who have granted the *Nihil Obstat* and *Imprimatur* agree with the contents, opinions, or statements expressed.

Every reasonable effort has been made to determine copyright holders of excerpted materials and to secure permissions as needed. If any copyrighted materials have been inadvertently used in this work without proper credit being given in one form or another, please notify Our Sunday Visitor in writing so that future printings of this work may be corrected accordingly.

Copyright © 2014 by Mitch Pacwa, S.J. Published 2014.

19 18 17 16 15 14   1 2 3 4 5 6 7 8 9

All rights reserved. With the exception of short excerpts for critical reviews, no part of this work may be reproduced or transmitted in any form or by any means whatsoever without permission in writing from the publisher. Contact: Our Sunday Visitor Publishing Division, Our Sunday Visitor, Inc., 200 Noll Plaza, Huntington, IN 46750; 1-800-348-2440; bookpermissions@osv.com.

ISBN: 978-1-61278-715-2 (Inventory No. T1419)
eISBN: 978-1-61278-314-7
LCCN: 2013956998

Cover design: Amanda Falk
Cover art: Shutterstock
Interior design: Sherri L. Hoffman
Interior art: iStockPhoto.com

PRINTED IN THE UNITED STATES OF AMERICA

To Fr. Rick Thomas, S.J.,
a great servant of the poor
who brought me back to daily praying the Rosary,
an inspiration for which I will be eternally grateful.

CONTENTS

How to Use This Study Guide in a Group   7

Acknowledgments   9

Introduction   11

Session 1 — Old Testament Background   17

Session 2 — The Annunciation   35

Session 3 — The Visitation to Elizabeth and the
    Annunciation to Joseph   51

Session 4 — The Birth and Infancy of Jesus   67

Session 5 — The Magi and Jesus' Childhood   87

Session 6 — Mary in Christ's Public Ministry   101

Session 7 — The "Woman" in John's Gospel   113

Session 8 — Mary After Jesus' Public Ministry   133

Session 9 — The Intercession of Mary   149

Marian Prayers   157

HOW TO USE THIS STUDY GUIDE IN A GROUP

This is an interactive study guide. It can be read with profit either alone or as part of a group Bible study. Below are suggestions for the use of this book in a group.

WHAT YOU WILL NEED FOR EVERY SESSION

- This study guide
- A Bible
- A notebook

- **Before Session 1, members of the group are encouraged to read the Introduction and Session 1 and to complete all the exercises in both.** They should bring this study guide with them to the group session.
- **Begin the session with prayer** (see "Marian Prayers" on page 157).
- **Invite one person in the group to read one of the Scripture passages included in this session's material.**
- **Allow five minutes of silent reflection on the passage.** This allows the group to quiet their inner thoughts and to center themselves on the lesson to be discussed.
- **Catechesis:** Give all members a chance to share some point that they have learned about Mary. Was this something new or a new insight into something? Was there anything that raised a question? (Allow fifteen to twenty minutes for this.)
- **Discussion:** Use the discussion questions at the end of the session chapter to begin a deeper grasp of the material covered in the session. (Allow fifteen to twenty minutes for this.)

- **Conclusion:** Have all members of the group summarize the key concepts they learned about Mary discussed in the session. Assign the next session as homework, to be completed before the next group session.

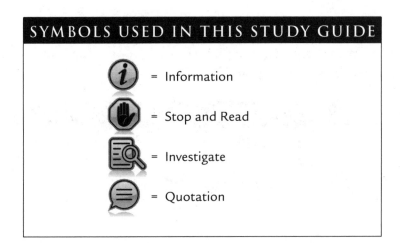

ACKNOWLEDGMENTS

Unless otherwise noted, the Scripture citations used in this work are taken from the *Catholic Edition of the Revised Standard Version of the Bible* (RSV), copyright © 1965, 1966 by the Division of Christian Education of the National Council of the Churches of Christ in the United States of America. Used by permission. All rights reserved. Where noted, other Scripture citations are from the *Revised Standard Version of the Bible — Second Catholic Edition* (Ignatius Edition), designated as RSV-SCE. Copyright © 2006 National Council of the Churches of Christ in the United States of America. Used by permission. All rights reserved.

Quotations from papal statements, Vatican II, and other Vatican documents are copyrighted, © 2014, Libreria Editrice Vaticana.

INTRODUCTION

> "We never give more honor to Jesus than when we honor his Mother, and we honor her simply and solely to honor him all the more perfectly. We go to her only as a way leading to the goal we seek — Jesus, her Son."
>
> — St. Louis Marie de Montfort

This book is a Bible study on the passages of the Old and New Testaments that have been particularly relevant to Marian doctrine over the centuries. The importance of these texts is that all Christians hold the Bible in common as a primary source of teaching, along with sacred Tradition, as Scripture itself teaches (2 Thess 2:15). I have two main goals in preparing this study that I'll go into a bit later, but first a little of my own story.

CONSIDER

Growing up in the Catholic faith in the 1950s and '60s included a lot of training in the teachings of the doctrines, morals, and pious practices that were meant to help us understand and live out the faith and morals. Among these were frequent teachings about saints who did marvelous and heroic things in their lives, with teachings about the Blessed Virgin Mary as the greatest of all saints.

Devotional practices and prayers — such as the Brown Scapular or May Crowning, but especially the Rosary — were normal components of Catholic life. Statues of the Blessed Mother were not only in church but in every classroom and most homes as well. Yet, at the same time, the *Baltimore Catechism* made it very clear in its teaching on the First Commandment that we may *worship* only God; we can *honor* the saints, especially the Blessed Virgin Mary, and use statues and pictures as helps to our prayer life.

THE FIRST COMMANDMENT

"199. What are we commanded by the first commandment?

"By the first commandment we are commanded to offer to God alone the supreme worship that is due Him.

"It is written, 'The Lord thy God shalt thou worship, and him only shalt thou serve' (Luke 4:8)."

— *Baltimore Catechism* (1941)

These teachings were obviously very important to the priests and nuns who taught us in church and school, and it was easy to see that they were sharing these elements from their own spiritual life.

When I entered Quigley North Preparatory Seminary in 1963 to begin my formal studies toward the priesthood, daily Mass and the Rosary, weekly confession, and three hours a day for homework were the bare minimum. The seminarian's prayer book we were required to purchase including devotions ranging around various issues in everyday Catholic life, with prominence given to Mass and the Marian devotions.

Of course, the Second Vatican Council was already under way, and it closed while I was still in high school. By the middle of my senior year, a translation of the documents of Vatican II came out, and they were used as our religion-class textbook in the second semester. These texts were dry reading, but they appeared to be in full continuity with the training I had already received, including Chapter VIII of *Lumen Gentium* (Dogmatic Constitution on the Church) on "Our Lady" (nn. 52-69), a teaching on the Blessed Virgin as the Mother of the Church.

However, it was not long after I had started college that changes were being made in the popular presentation on the Blessed Virgin. One of the concerns that was expressed was that Catholic devotions to Mary were offensive to Protestants, and since new and serious efforts toward ecumenical dialogue were being made, especially with the mainline denominations, Catholics would need to negotiate some points and even concede some issues.

> "This most Holy Synod deliberately teaches this Catholic doctrine and at the same time admonishes all the sons of the Church that the cult, especially the liturgical cult, of the Blessed Virgin, be generously fostered, and the practices and exercises of piety, recommended by the magisterium of the Church toward her in the course of centuries be made of great moment, and those decrees, which have been given in the early days regarding the cult of images of Christ, the Blessed Virgin and the saints, be religiously observed. But it exhorts theologians and preachers of the divine word to abstain zealously both from all gross exaggerations as well as from petty narrow-mindedness in considering the singular dignity of the Mother of God. Following the study of Sacred Scripture, the Holy Fathers, the doctors and liturgy of the Church, and under the guidance of the Church's magisterium, let them rightly illustrate the duties and privileges of the Blessed Virgin which always look to Christ, the source of all truth, sanctity and piety. Let them assiduously keep away from whatever, either by word or deed, could lead separated brethren or any other into error regarding the true doctrine of the Church. Let the faithful remember moreover that true devotion consists neither in sterile or transitory affection, nor in a certain vain credulity, but proceeds from true faith, by which we are led to know the excellence of the Mother of God, and we are moved to a filial love toward our mother and to the imitation of her virtues."
>
> — *Lumen Gentium* (n. 67)

Marian devotion was presented as one such negotiable. Praying the Rosary was no longer spoken about; homilies on Marian feast days highlighted her faith as a model to emulate but rarely mentioned her intercessory power. Images of Mary gradually began to disappear, even in some churches that previously had had "Mary altars" dedicated to her. I personally kept up my daily Rosary until late 1969, but it drifted away as I became busy working with street gangs in Chicago, and then with my philosophy and theology studies, and later high school teaching. This was not a conscious rejection but a neglect that caused a fading away.

Upon return from a mission trip to Peru in the summer of 1975, I took the bus from Mexico City to El Paso, Texas, to look up an old friend who had dropped out of sight after he returned from Vietnam. Since El Paso was his last address, I went there but never found him. Instead, at the Jesuit parish, Sacred Heart, I met Father Rick Thomas, S.J., with whom I spent an amazing few days. He was a leader in the Catholic Charismatic Renewal in El Paso and did fantastic work with extremely poor people living in the garbage dump across the Rio Grande River in Juarez, Mexico. He combined lively charismatic life with active social ministry, and I felt completely at home with this union of the spiritual life filled with faith and loving service to the poor.

One of the most long-lasting effects of that meeting was a ride to "The Lord's Ranch," a place for inner-city kids to get out into the country. The lasting effect came when he said, "You lead the Rosary." He did not ask if I wanted to pray it; he simply told me to lead it while he drove out to the ranch. Though a bit nervous because I had not prayed it in a few years, it all came right back to me because of good early training. I have not missed a day of praying the Rosary since then.

The mood in Catholic academic circles was not particularly open to Marian devotion, so I kept this practice, plus the renewed wearing of the Brown Scapular, generally to myself. However, I began to study Mariology, which is the theological study of Marian doctrine, for two reasons.

First, after having heard an anti-Catholic sermon on a local Protestant station, I volunteered to answer questions about the Catholic faith on that station's call-in radio show. Naturally, calls came in that were antagonistic to Marian devotion, but I was able to offer some answers to their objections by using the Bible, which I was then studying for my doctoral degree. This alerted me to the growing anti-Catholic literature coming from the likes of Jack Chick, Jimmy Swaggart, and hundreds of professional anti-Catholic organizations (for example, "Mission to Catholics") that had sprung up in the 1970s and later. To certain individuals, the Catholic Church's moves toward ecumenism were perceived as a weakness, which they were willing to seize by aggressive anti-Catholic literature and activity, making some publishers a lot of money in the process. It became important to answer their attacks and claims, which I did through radio programs, debates, and lectures.

The second reason for studying Mariology came while watching the Winter Olympics in Sarajevo in the former Yugoslavia. During a blizzard, the network filled in with a documentary they had prepared on some alleged apparitions of the Blessed Virgin to some teenagers in Medjugorje, Yugoslavia. A few years later I was invited to lead a couple of pilgrimage groups there and to appear in an ABC News documentary with the actively Catholic actor Martin Sheen. Along with visits to St. George Orthodox Church in Chicago, where an icon of the Blessed Virgin Mary in the iconostasis was apparently weeping oil from her eyes, my interest in Mary increased. Opportunities to lecture openly about Marian theology and devotion developed widely around the United States as large numbers of laity responded to Pope St. John Paul II's regular inclusion of the Blessed Virgin in his prayers, in the

"It gives great joy and comfort to this holy and general Synod that even among the separated brethren there are some who give due honor to the Mother of our Lord and Savior, especially among the Orientals, who with devout mind and fervent impulse give honor to the Mother of God, ever virgin. The entire body of the faithful pours forth instant supplications to the Mother of God and Mother of men that she, who aided the beginnings of the Church by her prayers, may now, exalted as she is above all the angels and saints, intercede before her Son in the fellowship of all the saints, until all families of people, whether they are honored with the title of Christian or whether they still do not know the Savior, may be happily gathered together in peace and harmony into one people of God, for the glory of the Most Holy and Undivided Trinity."

— *Lumen Gentium* (n. 69)

dedication of each country he visited to her, and in his teachings on her, particularly in his encyclical *Redemptoris Mater* ("Mother of the Redeemer"). Which brings me to my reasons for writing this study.

First, ecumenical dialogue. Dialogue with Protestants is extremely important. Since most of their denominations accept the Bible alone (*sola scriptura*) as the source of doctrine, it is essential to engage them in dialogue with Sacred Scripture regarding Mary. Most of them have vague knowledge of the Marian passages, and extremely rarely will they hear a sermon on these texts that are meant to honor Mary. They tend to fear Catholic doctrine; and if they preach about these texts, it is to refute or reject Catholic teachings by minimizing the Blessed Mother's importance: she is just an ordinary woman, no different from any other woman.

My second goal is to nourish Catholic Marian devotion. This is the far more important reason. Marian teaching advances best when it is grounded in a sensitive reading of the scriptural text. Similarly, Marian devotion is best nourished by the bread that "proceeds out of the mouth of the LORD" (Deut 8:3) — namely, the word of God. Understanding this is key to growing in love for Mary.

THE ROSARY AND SCRIPTURE

Praying the Rosary includes the recitation of the Our Fathers, Hail Marys, and Glory Be's as its body, but meditation on each of the twenty mysteries of the Rosary is its soul (Paul VI, *Marialis Cultus* [for the right ordering and development of devotion to the Blessed Virgin Mary], n. 47; St. John Paul II, *Rosarium Virginis Mariae* ["Rosary of the Virgin Mary"], n. 12). Such meditation is well nourished on Sacred Scripture.

Session 1

OLD TESTAMENT BACKGROUND

> "The books of the Old Testament describe the history of salvation, by which the coming of Christ into the world was slowly prepared. These earliest documents, as they are read in the Church and are understood in the light of a further and full revelation, bring the figure of the woman, Mother of the Redeemer, into a gradually clearer light."
>
> — *Lumen Gentium* (n. 55)

Certainly many prophecies in the Old Testament prepare the way for Mary, and a number of women and images prefigure the Blessed Virgin. We cannot deal with all of them, but two images are absolutely key to the New Testament image of the Blessed Virgin Mary and should be studied before the New Testament texts are addressed.

The most important text comes at the beginning of Scripture — the creation of the first woman and her role in the history of salvation. Her role takes place in a context that includes a number of important ideas that recur in the New Testament with regard to a variety of topics. We will limit our interests here to key links with Mary and Jesus.

 Stop here and read **Genesis 2:15-3:24** in your own Bible.

Two dramatic issues are addressed after the Lord God makes Adam. The first is the giving of the one and only commandment by the Lord God (Gen 2:15-17) — the commandment forbidding eating from the tree of the knowledge of good and evil.

The second is Adam's social nature, which the Lord God recognizes before Adam does. In Genesis 2:18-20, the Lord God teases Adam a bit by forming a variety of animals and birds. Most boys (including this author) would consider it very cool to have elephants, horses, lions, tigers — and, of course, dogs — as pets.

The man certainly shows one element of his distinctiveness in that he names all the animals; they do not name him. This indicates that he is made in the image and likeness of God (Gen 1:26-27), both in the fact that his capacity to name shows that he has a reasoning, thinking capacity like God's, and in the fact that he has dominion over the animals. The Lord God creates the animals for the sake of the human being, who was himself created for his own sake. Nonetheless, however good the animals might be, they are not suitable partners for the man since they cannot be his equals, so God takes the initiative to find a suitable helper for the man.

ADAM AS HUMAN BEING

Adam means "man" in Hebrew, in the sense of human being rather than as a male. It is derived from a root word meaning "red," from which is also derived the word for the ground — *adamah*. Since much of soil has a reddish tint, and so do many humans, this term is used. "Human" is also a very appropriate term since its Latin root is derived from the term "humus," meaning "soil," and thereby forms a nice parallel with the Hebrew terms.

The Lord's solution to the man's aloneness is to fashion a woman.

INVESTIGATE

 Look up the following passages and make notes on the creation of Eve:

PASSAGE	NOTES
Genesis 2:21-22	
Genesis 2:23-25	
Genesis 2:24-25	

STUDY

Key to the understanding of these passages is the statement that "they become one flesh," which indicates yet another way in which humans are created in the image and likeness of God: they are capable of a communion with a fellow person. Just as Father, Son, and Holy Spirit form a communion of three equally, fully divine Persons in the one Godhead, so can humans become an image of selfless love as self-gift and as acceptance of another person.

> "Indeed, the Lord Jesus, when He prayed to the Father, 'that all may be one ... as we are one' (Jn 17:21-22) opened up vistas closed to human reason, for He implied a certain likeness between the union of the divine Persons, and the unity of God's sons in truth and charity. This likeness reveals that man, who is the only creature on earth which God willed for itself, cannot fully find himself except through a sincere gift of himself."
>
> — *Gaudium et Spes* (Pastoral Constitution on the Church in the Modern World, n. 24)

This aspect of intercommunion between Adam and the woman ought to be remembered when considering the role of the Blessed Virgin Mary in the history of salvation. God chose the incarnation of the Son as the way to redeem the human race, and this would take place in Mary's womb. However, this mystery cannot be understood without seeing that she who was full of grace was thereby in a relationship of communion with God. At the Incarnation, she will accept God's offer and enter into a communion with Christ, the New Adam, who dwells in her womb and then in her home. The roles of Jesus the New Adam and Mary the New Eve will be complementary in the history of salvation, and the Christian does well to pay attention to this complementarity.

The idyllic quality of the garden is described in the couple's lack of shame in their nakedness. This implies that neither sought to use the other for selfish reasons such as lust, which would augment the lack of shame. Into this idyllic state comes the subtle serpent, who engages the woman in a dialogue of temptation that obscures truth from her.

INVESTIGATE

THE TEMPTATION

 Look up the following passage and make notes on the temptation:

PASSAGE	NOTES
Genesis 3:1-5	

STUDY

The serpent begins with a question about the one commandment
that the Lord God had given to Adam, asking if God really made
such a command. It is important to note that the temptation comes
from outside of the woman — that is, the serpent asks her. Since
she has not yet fallen into sin and does not yet have the disorder it
causes, her temptation is external. This will be an important aspect
in understanding the lack of original sin in Jesus Christ and in Mary.

The woman knows the commandment, as seen by her ability to
repeat it to the serpent, which means she had learned it from Adam.
However, note that she adds that they may not even touch the tree, a
point that the original commandment had not contained.

Famously, the serpent denies the punishment and then imputes
jealousy to God's motives in verses 4 and 5. Only at this point does
Eve look at the tree without fear of death and find it physically attrac-
tive, "good for food" and "a delight to the eyes," as well as "desired
to make one wise" (Gen 3:6). The temptation gave her the idea of
eating, which she then turned into action, not only for herself but
also for her husband, who silently stood next to her. Adam's sin was

not only the act of disobedience in eating the fruit but also his silent inaction to combat the temptation.

INVESTIGATE

ORIGINAL SIN AND ITS CONSEQUENCES

 Look up the following passages and make notes on original sin and its consequences:

PASSAGE	NOTES
Genesis 3:7-13	
Genesis 3:14-15	
Genesis 3:16-19	
Genesis 3:20-24	

CONSIDER

The result of the sin was that Adam and Eve now knew both good and evil instead of good alone. Their eyes were opened to seeing their nakedness and realizing their shame. This was not only embarrassment at self-exposure but also the possibility of selfish desires to use each other as objects, which would become a staple component of human history through the violence, lust, and enslavement that persist to the present time.

The Lord God came to the garden, which led the first humans to hide from him among the trees from which they had once freely eaten. While the humans hide, the Lord seeks them, asking, "Where are you?" (Gen 3:9). This question becomes a key to understanding the whole Bible: the Lord God is looking for humans; they are often not simply avoiding the search for him but actively hide from him. However, the Lord will eventually seek out Abram, Moses, Samuel, David, the prophets and apostles, and one day, the Blessed Virgin Mary.

Once the man admits that he was hiding because he was naked, the Lord asks other questions: "Who told you that you were naked? Have you eaten of the tree of which I commanded you not to eat?" The responses are not very direct, since both man and woman want to shift the blame. Adam says, "The woman whom you gave to be with me, she gave me fruit of the tree, and I ate." Note that not only is the woman at fault for giving him the fruit, but so also is God, who gave her to Adam in the first place. The woman answered God's question by blaming the serpent: "The serpent beguiled me, and I ate" (Gen 3:11, 12, 13 — RSV-SCE).

The Lord responds to these excuses and lame admissions of guilt by pronouncing three punishments.

First, he curses the serpent, which is bad news for the serpent. However, the second part of the curse contains hope and promise for human beings: "I will put enmity between you and the woman, and between your seed and her seed; he shall bruise your head, and you shall bruise his heel" (Gen 3:15).

This enmity between the serpent and the woman is beyond the

natural recoil in the presence of snakes, particularly poisonous ones. There will be enmity and mutual attacks that will echo throughout human history until the end of time. In Revelation 12:3-4, John saw a vision of a "great red dragon" who "stood before the woman who was about to bear a child, that he might devour her child when she brought it forth." The dragon is then identified as "that ancient serpent, who is called the Devil and Satan, the deceiver of the whole world" (Rev 12:9).

Second, the Lord punishes the woman by causing pain in childbirth and having husbands rule over their wives. While some men look to this as a biblical warrant for having power over their wives, their boast is quite misplaced: their rule is the wives' punishment for breaking God's commandment, not a reward. Such boasting would be like a prison wall bragging that it keeps inmates inside.

Third, the Lord punishes Adam for listening to his wife's suggestion to eat the fruit. The implication is that he should have said "no" to her, rather than cooperate with the sin. Therefore, the ground is cursed to the point of forcing him to toil against its thorns and thistles and sweat to eat his food. The conclusion is that he will die and return to the ground (*adamah*) from which he was taken.

Only after the Lord God decrees his punishments of the perpetrators of temptation and disobedience does Adam call his wife "Eve" (Hebrew, *Havah*; Greek Septuagint, *Zoe*), a word derived from an old form of the Hebrew word for life.

Finally, God banishes Adam and Eve from the garden and places a cherubim with a flaming sword at its entrance. The cherubim's flaming sword would be lowered after a soldier used his sword to pierce the side of the New Adam on the new Tree of Life, the cross set up in another garden west of Jerusalem, in the presence of Mary, the New Eve.

CONSIDER

A very odd phrase in Genesis 3:15 says that the enmity will be "between your seed and her seed." The serpent is depicted as masculine, so there is no problem with speaking of his seed. However, since the "seed" always refers to the man's contribution to the conception of a child, one must ask how the woman can have "seed"? This would have perplexed the ancients, and most modern people ignore it. However, in light of Jesus' virginal conception in the womb of the Blessed Virgin Mary, this promise takes on a new importance. No male seed was introduced to Mary's womb to conceive her child; only her child can be identified as a woman's seed. Therefore he will be the seed that crushes the ancient serpent's head in a thorough defeat. For this reason, this passage is frequently identified as the "Proto-Gospel," the first proclamation of what Christ, the Son of God and Son of the Virgin, will accomplish for the human race that fell into sin with Adam and Eve's sin. As *Lumen Gentium* (n. 55) says, "[Mary] is already prophetically foreshadowed in the promise of victory over the serpent which was given to our first parents after their fall into sin (cf. Gen 3:15)."

CONFLICTING TRANSLATIONS?

Why does the Vulgate say, "She will crush his head" while modern translations say, "He will crush his head"?

The Hebrew (*hu'*) and the Greek Septuagint (*autos*) clearly read the masculine pronoun here. However, the thirteenth-century Paris manuscript of the Latin Vulgate reads *ipsa* (she), and that was the manuscript used for the Clementine edition and the Douay-Rheims Catholic English translation of the Bible. However, earlier manuscripts read *ipse* (he). We will follow the Hebrew, Greek, and earlier Latin manuscripts by reading "he," which makes this line of Genesis focused on Christ.

STUDY

The New Testament draws a number of points from the story of Adam and Eve that we need to consider in light of the Blessed Virgin.

First, all humanity descends from this first pair, and their original sin is inherited by humanity, with only Jesus Christ and his

Blessed Mother excepted. Some argue that this is unfair, yet the reality of sin affecting those who did not commit it is a common human experience. Consider the effects of the terrorists on 9/11 and other attempts to blow up airplanes. Today billions of dollars are spent annually around the world on security screening that was not necessary before those attacks. Every since the "shoe bomber" attempt, passengers must screen their shoes before boarding planes. Because a woman tried to sneak explosives onto a plane in her baby's bottles, liquids are limited on planes. This and many other sinful behaviors of a wide variety have affected everyone else. Why should anyone be surprised that the sin of Adam and Eve would affect all of their descendants?

The teaching of universal fallenness through original sin lies behind the New Testament's teaching for the need of redemption.

INVESTIGATE

REDEMPTION

Look up the following passages and make notes on sin and the need for forgiveness:

PASSAGE	NOTES
Ecclesiastes 7:20	
Romans 3:9-10	

Romans 3:23	
Romans 11:32	
1 John 1:8-10	

Another important point made in the New Testament is that Jesus Christ is the New Adam who undoes the sin and punishment of the first Adam.

INVESTIGATE

THE NEW ADAM

Look up the following passages and make notes on Jesus as the New Adam:

PASSAGE	NOTES
Romans 5:12-19	

1 Corinthians 15:20-22	
1 Corinthians 15:45-49	

STUDY

The New Testament and the Fathers of the Church will begin to see Mary as the New Eve in parallel to Jesus Christ the New Adam. This will become an important development in the Church's teaching on the importance of the Blessed Virgin Mary in salvation history, so we will examine the passages and the patristic teachings that deal with this theme.

The Eastern Churches often take a mystical and poetic approach to seeing typologies in the Old Testament for the New. One example of this is the burning bush as an image of the Virgin Mary.

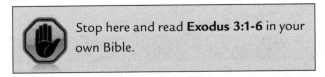

Stop here and read **Exodus 3:1-6** in your own Bible.

Just as the presence of God in the bush appeared as a "flame of fire" (Gen 3:2) and yet did not consume the bush, so also did the presence of the Holy Spirit overshadow the Virgin Mary, and God the Son was conceived in her womb without destroying her. The presence of God evokes fear because his holiness is so powerful (see also Gen 17:3; Judg 13:22; 1 Kings 19:11-13). It is useful to note that the Hebrew word for "holy" (*qadosh*) comes from a root meaning "to be on fire" and "to be separate" (from the secular and vain). The sense of God's holiness as a purifying flame can also be understood as a destroying flame to the wicked. However, when the Lord God dwells within the womb of the Virgin Mary, he does not destroy her but lets her live and preserves her virginity even as the bush on Horeb, the "mountain of God," is preserved intact.

"BURNING BUSH" IMAGERY

St. Ephrem the Syrian used the imagery of the burning bush in his "Hymns on the Nativity," and the idea entered the writings of other Fathers of the Church after him. Therefore, this passage and St. Stephen's inclusion of the episode in his trial speech (Acts 7:30-34) are used in the liturgies on the feasts of the Blessed Virgin in the Eastern Rites.

Closely related to the burning bush is the Ark of the Covenant, as an image of the Virgin Mary. This may have been suggested by the appearance of the Ark of the Covenant in Revelation 11:19: "Then God's temple in heaven was opened, and the ark of his covenant was seen within his temple," immediately before the vision of the woman clothed with the sun, who gives birth to Christ. Yet it has its own qualities that evoke a parallelism with the Virgin Mary that is seen in passages that deal with the history of the ark.

 Stop here and read **Exodus 25:10-21** and **40:34-38** in your own Bible.

The first passage (Ex 25:10-21) focuses on a description of the Ark of the Covenant. A cubit is the length from one's elbow to middle fingertip — about one and a half feet — so therefore the ark was about 45 inches long, 27 inches wide, and 27 inches high. It was made of acacia wood, a light, very durable wood common to Sinai, and the Negev desert, with a gold overlay. Inside it contained the "testimony" — that is, the Ten Commandments. On top of the ark was the "mercy seat," a covering of pure gold, with a cherub at each end, facing each other, with wings spread over the mercy seat. The cherubim protected the "testimony" inside the ark, just as they protected the Tree of Life (Gen 3:24).

The ark was considered a symbol of the Virgin Mary because she carried the new Testimony, the unborn Word of God made flesh, within her womb. As such, she became a vehicle of God's presence in a much more realistic way than the acacia wood ark of the Old Covenant.

The second important passage (Ex 40:34-38) describes the cloud that covered the tent of meeting when the Ark of the Covenant was placed in it. A number of Church Fathers have seen this as an image of the overshadowing of the Holy Spirit when the Word became flesh in Mary's womb at the Annunciation (Lk 1:35).

CONSIDER

Two other sets of narratives about the history of the Ark of the Covenant appear in 1 and 2 Samuel. 1 Samuel 4-6 tells about the punishment against the high priest Eli and his sons Hophni and Phinehas (which are names from the Egyptian language). When the sons brought the ark to battle, the Philistines killed them, took the ark, and Eli died of a stroke or heart attack in Shiloh. The Philistines tried to keep the ark as a prize of their own pride, but they were punished with plagues and let it return to Israel. When it came to Beth-shemesh on a Philistine oxcart, the people looked inside of it and died, since they were not priests and were not eligible to touch it. They sent the ark to Kiriath-jearim, a few miles northeast of Beth-shemesh, where it peacefully remained until King David brought it to Jerusalem. Today, at the hilltop site of the threshing floor of Abinadab (in Kiriath-jearim, west of Jerusalem), stands the Church of Our Lady of the Ark of the Covenant.

It is also worth looking at 2 Samuel 6:2-7, where David brings up the ark. David had the ark brought out on a new cart. When the oxen that were carrying it stumbled, a man named Uzzah touched the ark, trying to steady it. God "smote" Uzzah and killed him on the spot. This part of the narrative seems very odd and even unfair: Uzzah was trying to prevent the ark from falling off the cart; why would God punish him? However, in Exodus it was clear that the ark should be carried by the priests using gold-covered poles (25:12-15) and not on a cart. Nor should a layman, a soldier, be protecting the ark. It was too sacred for him to touch with impunity. David had politicized the ark and was bringing it to Jerusalem to show that this was now his capital. This explains his rhetorical question in Samuel 6:9: "How can the ark of the LORD come to me?" After six months of staying at a nearby place, David continued the process of bringing the ark to Jerusalem. But notice how 2 Samuel 6:12-14 describes it:

> David went and brought up the ark of God from the house of Obed-edom to the city of David with rejoicing; and when those who bore the ark of the LORD had gone six paces, he sacrificed an ox and a fatling. And David danced before the LORD with all his might; and David was girded with a linen ephod.

This is made clearer in 1 Chronicles 15:2 when David said, "No one but the Levites may carry the ark of God, for the LORD chose them to carry the ark of the LORD and to minister to him for ever."

These passages indicate the sacredness of the Ark of the Covenant, which would not be placed under the control of human beings who tried to manipulate it for their own military, political, or other worldly purposes. So, too, the Virgin Mary belongs in a special way to God's sacred purposes, especially the bearing of his only-begotten Son, Jesus Christ.

STUDY

Another important Old Testament reference to Mary occurs in Isaiah 7:10-17, which prophesies that a virgin will conceive. To understand this passage, we need a little background.

The mid-730s B.C. were a time of crisis, when the king of Assyria, Tiglath Pileser III, was attacking western Asia, and Syria, Philistia, Tyre, Sidon, and Israel formed an alliance to protect themselves. Judah did not join, so Syria and the Northern Kingdom of Israel invaded Judah in order to replace King Ahaz and force Judah into the anti-Assyrian alliance. In the face of this crisis, Isaiah asked King Ahaz of Judah to choose some sign by which God would show that Judah would be protected. However, Isaiah ended up giving the sign to him, since Ahaz was afraid to make such an act of faith.

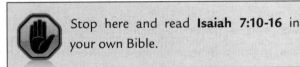

Stop here and read **Isaiah 7:10-16** in your own Bible.

Isaiah took the initiative to invite Ahaz to choose any sign of the Lord's fulfillment that he could think of. However, he refused to do so out of a false piety that claimed he did not want to "test" the Lord. Certainly, Moses taught in Deuteronomy 6:16, "You shall not put the LORD your God to the test," but Ahaz certainly tested the Lord in various ways, such as sacrificing his sons to a pagan deity in the Valley of Hinnom (in Aramaic, "Gehenna") to avoid an attack (2 Chron 28:1-4).

In the face of Ahaz's lack of faith, Isaiah chose the sign of God's salvation for Judah: Immanuel. The sign is described in Isaiah 7:14b: "Behold, a young woman [*almah*] shall conceive and bear a son, and shall call his name Immanuel."

A good deal of controversy surrounds this verse, so it is worth looking at the ancient words and translations. The Hebrew word *almah* can refer to any young woman before she gives birth to a child. However, the Greek Septuagint translation (probably the second century B.C.) translates *almah* with the word *parthenos*, which specifically means a "virgin," and the Aramaic Targum also uses the word *bethultha* to mean "virgin." These translations indicate that Jewish readers understood *almah* in the sense of "virgin," and this is the background for citing this verse in Matthew 1:23, where it shows that Mary's virginal conception of Jesus by the power of the Holy Spirit was the fulfillment of this prophecy.

"Immanuel" (derived from Hebrew) is simply "God (*El*) is with us (*immanu*)." The child will indicate through his name that God is present with the people during this grave political crisis, so neither the king nor the people need fear.

CONSIDER

The history of the human race since the fall of Adam and Eve has been one of sin, even among the best of people. However, it is precisely for sinners that God the Son "became flesh and dwelt among us" (Jn 1:14). Yet, how does the Son enter this polluted river of the history of universal sin without becoming contaminated? One key to that answer is his incarnation in the womb of the Immaculate Virgin Mary.

Venerable Archbishop Fulton Sheen used an image that appealed to my roots in Chicago when he compared the Virgin Mary to a lock on a river. The city of Chicago used the Chicago River as its sewer system, even into my adolescent years. One big problem used to be that the river flowed into Lake Michigan, the city's source of fresh drinking water. To fix this problem, a canal was dug to another river, lower in altitude. The final barricade was destroyed, and the Chicago River reversed its course, flowing away from Lake Michigan's fresh water to unfortunate cities and towns downstate. Then a lock was placed where the lake flowed into the Chicago River, preventing polluted river water from entering the lake water, and so it remains until the present (though now the river is much cleaner).

The immaculate and sinless Virgin Mary is the lock through whom the infinite reservoir of God's grace in Christ Jesus flows into the polluted human race — which does not clean up so easily as the Chicago River.

DISCUSS

1. What new insights into the story of Adam and Eve have you gained from looking at the account of the temptation and the serpent in the Genesis passages?

2. How is Mary like the burning bush? How is she like the Ark of the Covenant? In what way do these images help you understand Mary's role in our lives?
3. Do you ever experience the desire to shift blame for your actions to someone else, as Adam and Eve did? How does this temptation lead to greater sin?

PRACTICE

This week, consider how the titles we give to Mary reflect what we believe about Mary and her part in the history of salvation. Read the Litany of the Blessed Virgin Mary on page 158 and see how many titles have Old Testament roots. Choose one title that has particular meaning for you, and keep that image in mind as you pray the Hail Mary.

Session 2

THE ANNUNCIATION

"Adorned from the first instant of her conception with the radiance of an entirely unique holiness, the Virgin of Nazareth is greeted, on God's command, by an angel messenger as 'full of grace' (cf. Lk 1:28), and to the heavenly messenger she replies: 'Behold the handmaid of the Lord, be it done unto me according to thy word' (Lk 1:38). Thus Mary, a daughter of Adam, consenting to the divine Word, became the mother of Jesus, the one and only Mediator. Embracing God's salvific will with a full heart and impeded by no sin, she devoted herself totally as a handmaid of the Lord to the person and work of her Son, under Him and with Him, by the grace of almighty God, serving the mystery of redemption."

— *Lumen Gentium* (n. 56)

Luke begins his Gospel with a prologue that describes his purpose and task. The style is excellent, and much of his writing shows evidence of great Greek style and richness of vocabulary. However, the rest of Luke 1 and 2 betrays a poorer quality of Greek. In fact, it is full of Aramaisms — that is, words and phrases that make better sense and style in Aramaic than they do in Greek. For this reason, a number of scholars suggest that these passages were translated by Luke from an Aramaic original. He preserves elements that Greek stylists would consider barbaric but which at the same time keep the flavor of the Semitic background of the scenes. However, this evidence does not prove that the Blessed Mother had personally explained these things to Luke, as is sometimes believed. It makes more literary sense that he had been given a written Aramaic text whose language style he preserved. However, the Church has always considered that the witness underlying these episodes would have been the Blessed Virgin Mary, the only witness of these events who survived Pentecost. Her words to the early apostles and disciples are the source and indicate her influence on Sacred Scripture and some important aspects of the life of Jesus and the salvation of the world.

The first event concerning the Blessed Virgin Mary is the scene where the angel Gabriel approaches her to say that she will bear a son by the power of the Holy Spirit, without the natural cooperation of a man. This scene parallels the annunciation of the birth of John the Baptist to his father, the priest Zechariah, by the same angel Gabriel.

The introductory verses (1:26-27) set the scene.

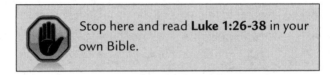

Stop here and read **Luke 1:26-38** in your own Bible.

The time reference (sixth month) is made in relation to the conception of John the Baptist. As with the elderly Zechariah and Elizabeth, Mary and her betrothed Joseph are introduced as expecting no child, though their reason is that they are engaged but not living together. Also, Joseph's Davidic lineage is mentioned now but will play a role later when it is time for Jesus to be born.

When the angel Gabriel enters Mary's presence, he addresses her as "O favored one." Angels are messengers from God who deliver precisely the message that God wants to communicate. In this case, Gabriel addresses the Virgin Mary not by name but with a description of her relationship with God. This is quite distinctive, when one considers that usually other people are greeted by name when angels appear — including Abram, Moses, Daniel, and Zechariah. In a few cases, the angel of the Lord uses a descriptive title:

- Judges 6:12: "The LORD is with you, you mighty man of valor," an angel said to Gideon.

- Daniel 10:19: The angel addressed Daniel, "O man greatly beloved."

However, the greeting to Mary is quite distinctive in that it focuses on what the Lord is doing within her and on his presence with her.

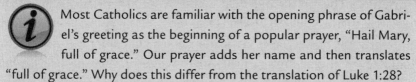

"FULL OF GRACE"

Most Catholics are familiar with the opening phrase of Gabriel's greeting as the beginning of a popular prayer, "Hail Mary, full of grace." Our prayer adds her name and then translates "full of grace." Why does this differ from the translation of Luke 1:28?

The Greek word translated as "favored one" is *kecharitomene*, a perfect passive participle in the feminine singular form. The root, *charitoo*, is very rare in secular Greek and appears in the New Testament only here and in Ephesians 1:6. It means to "show favor" or "give grace." The Hebrew word for grace also means "favor," so some people like the translation "favored one," but it seems preferable to use the term "graced one" as a way to indicate that the power of God's grace, and not mere favoritism, is at stake.

St. Jerome translated this expression as "full of grace," as does the Syriac translation of this verse. This is an idiomatic translation based on the way Greek speakers had explained its meaning to a Latin speaker (St. Jerome).

CONSIDER

The angel's greeting has led the Church to reflect on Mary, the person to whom it was directed. Therefore, Vatican II teaches:

> It is no wonder therefore that the usage prevailed among the Fathers whereby they called the mother of God entirely holy and free from all stain of sin, as though fashioned by the Holy Spirit and formed as a new creature. Adorned from the first instant of her conception with the radiance of an entirely unique holiness, the Virgin of Nazareth is greeted, on God's command,

by an angel messenger as "full of grace" (cf. Lk 1:28). (*Lumen Gentium*, n. 56)

As this states, the angel's greeting is a first step in the Church's understanding that Mary was conceived without sin. Mary is troubled by the angel's greeting that addresses her as "graced one" and announces that the Lord is with her. The Greek root of the word "troubled" means to "shake," "stir up," and figuratively "disturb," "unsettle." The prefix *dia* before this word intensifies it to mean "greatly" disturb, which also has the sense of "perplex." When Mary is greatly perplexed here, it leads her to "consider" — or better, "ponder" — the meaning of this sort of greeting (the phrase "in her mind" is not in Greek, though a few manuscripts read "within herself"). Being "graced" and having the Lord with her does not mean that she understands everything happening to her. However, God's presence does prevent her from dismissing the words as unimportant. Rather, her lack of understanding draws her into deeper contemplation, a pattern that will reappear later in Luke.

The angel addresses her unspoken pondering with the content of the message he was sent to bring.

The first part of the message is concerned with Mary herself. The initial command, "Fear not" (or "Do not be afraid") is typical of the opening of messages given to human beings by the Lord and his angels. Mary is told not to be afraid on the basis that she has found "favor" — or better, "grace" — with God. No such reason to cease fearing the presence of God or his angels is ever given in the Old Testament.

INVESTIGATE

"FEAR NOT" (NO. 1)

 Look up the following passages and make notes on the angelic messages:

PASSAGE	NOTES
Genesis 32:30	
Exodus 33:20	
Jeremiah 1:8	
Ezekiel 2:6	
Ezekiel 3:9	
Matthew 28:5	
Luke 1:13	

Acts 18:9	
Acts 27:24	

STUDY

The second part of the angel's message is the central point and purpose of his visit: the announcement of the birth of a son. The emphatic point that "you will conceive [him] in your womb" (Lk 1:31) makes it clear that he will not be adopted. Also, this will stand in stark contrast to various pagan stories of gods taking human shape; those gods never go through the human gestation process but merely look like human beings for a short time (usually to work mischief with people), and then they resume their divine shape to escape the harmful consequences of their mischief. This part of the message makes it clear that Mary's child will truly take on human nature.

DOCETISM

One type of heresy in the early Church was Docetism, a word derived from the Greek word *dokeo* meaning "to seem, appear." This doctrine believed that it was below God's dignity to truly take on human flesh, so Docetists taught that the Son only seemed to become human. As with the pagan myths, it was merely the appearance of human nature.

The third part of the angel's message is a multipart description of the Son: he will be the Son of the Most High; he will be given David's throne, and he will reign forever.

Like John the Baptist, Jesus will be "great." Later, John will proclaim that Jesus is greater than he: "[H]e who is mightier than I is coming, the thong of whose sandals I am not worthy to untie" (Lk 3:16).

In Luke 1:31, Mary is instructed to call him Jesus, where "call" is a very Semitic idiom. In this verse, the verb "call" is in the active voice, indicating that this is Mary's action. The meaning of the name Jesus is not explained here, perhaps because this text was origi-

THE MOST HIGH

"Most High" is a Semitic title for God, found in Ugaritic texts in regard to the chief Canaanite deity, *'il 'ilyn*, as well as in the Old Testament. Melchizedek worships God Most High (*El Elyon*) in Genesis 14:18-20, 22; Balaam in Numbers 24:16; Moses in Deuteronomy 32:8 ("the Most High gave to the nations their inheritance"); frequently in Daniel when speaking with Babylonians and of the final judgment in Daniel 7:18, 22, 25, 27; and most often in the Psalms.

Two interesting kinds of uses occur when Israelites are in conversation with gentiles (Melchizedek, Balaam, Babylonian kings). In those cases, "God Most High" is used as a bridge between Israelite ideas of God and the pagans, who do not recognize the Lord, but have a "Most High God." If that aspect is present here, then the name "Most High God" is a way to connect his Son with the redemption of the gentiles.

The second aspect is the use in Daniel 7:18, 22, 25, 27, where the Most High is the judge of his people and the "son of man" appears as the one to whom "was given dominion and glory and kingdom, that all peoples, nations, and languages should serve him; his dominion is an everlasting dominion, which shall not pass away, and his kingdom one that shall not be destroyed" (Dan 7:13-14).

This takes place in the context of the great battle against the apocalyptic beasts and their final judgment and links the kingdom of the Son of man with his title of Son of the Most High, and the promise that his kingdom will have no end. However, it also provides a background to the role of the woman in Revelation 12, who gives birth to a son destined to rule the nations while the red dragon fights against both son and mother.

41

nally in Hebrew or Aramaic and the name needed no explanation to readers of either language. Only in the narration of Joseph's dream, where he is told to name the child "Jesus" does Matthew explain its connection to the Hebrew root meaning "save."

While Mary is actively to call him Jesus, in verse 32 it says in passive voice, "he … will be called," an idiom frequently designated a "divine passive." The passive form of speech is commonly used in the Bible to indicate something that God will accomplish. Here it indicates that God will identify him as his own Son. Human beings do not have the power to make anyone divine, but God can recognize the identity of his own Son, as we see in Luke 10:22: "[N]o one knows who the Son is except the Father."

STUDY

The phrase "The Lord God will give to him the throne of his father David" (Lk 1:32) connects the announcement of this child's birth with the Old Testament promises of a Messiah from the family of David. The beginning of these promises was the prophet Nathan's word to David in 2 Samuel 7:12-13:

> When your days are fulfilled and you lie down with your fathers, I will raise up your offspring after you, who shall come forth from your body, and I will establish his kingdom. He shall build a house for my name, and I will establish the throne of his kingdom for ever.

In the angel Gabriel's words to Mary, the promise now comes to its fulfillment, if she accepts her role.

INVESTIGATE

THE DAVIDIC PROMISE

Look up the following passages and make notes on what the Psalms say about the Messiah and the Davidic promise:

PASSAGE	NOTES
Psalm 2:7	
Psalm 27	
Psalm 89:26	
Psalm 132:11	

Gabriel elaborates on the Davidic promise by saying that the child "will reign over the house of Jacob for ever" (Lk 1:33). The idea that the child will "reign" is yet another extension of the messianic promise. The earliest expression that the Messiah will come from the tribe of Judah is Jacob's blessing to Judah in Genesis 49:10: "The scepter shall not depart from Judah, nor the ruler's staff from between his feet, until he comes to whom it belongs; and to him shall be the obedience of the peoples."

Another significant phrase is "house of Jacob," which represents the whole of Israel. Solomon had died after much foolish behavior, and his son and successor, Rehoboam, was a bigger fool, whose policies led to the split of the nation into two kingdoms: Israel in the north and Judah in the south. However, this phrase promises that Mary's child will reign over the whole house of Jacob, the father of the northern and southern tribes alike. Isaiah was especially fond of speaking of the whole nation as "the house of Jacob," but the expression appears first in Exodus. This verse in Luke is the only New Testament use of the phrase.

MARY AND THE PUBLIC PROCLAMATION OF JESUS' KINGSHIP

Only once during Jesus' earthly life did Mary see him announced as King of the Jews — while he hung upon the cross. Although the announcement of his conception evoked a tremendous amount of faith from Mary, the sign above his head as he hung on the cross became yet another challenge to her faith. As a young woman hearing Gabriel's words about the Messiah's eternal kingdom, many standard images of magnificence and rule would naturally come to her from the Old Testament. None of those images could have prepared the mature mother as she watched her son die on the cross.

Gabriel then concludes his message by saying, "and of his kingdom there will be no end" (Lk 1:33). The key here is that the angel Gabriel announces that the kingdom without end is about to begin in the womb of Mary. It is her response to this annunciation and its implied call that he awaits.

Mary responds with a question in the next verse: "How shall this be, since I have no husband?" Mary does not seek evidence but wants to know how the promised child can be conceived since she does not "know man" (a more literal translation than "I have no husband"), a Semitic expression for sexual relations. This confirms the earlier statement that she was still only betrothed to Joseph and not yet living with him as his wife. The angel responds to Mary's question with an explanation that she will conceive by the Holy Spirit. Then he adds proof of God's power by offering a sign, even though

Mary did not ask for a sign — telling her that her elderly kinswoman Elizabeth has conceived a son. This, however, will not be evidence that she clings to but will become a motive to go to Elizabeth.

The central point of Gabriel's answer is the Holy Spirit, whom he identifies as the "power of the Most High" (Lk 1:35). In Luke 1:32, he identifies Mary's child as the "Son of the Most High," and then he says that the Holy Spirit is the Most High's power. In these verses, we see that the Most High, his Son, and his Holy Spirit are intimately connected in full cooperation to bring about the miraculous conception of a son in Mary's womb. At the same time, each of them is mentioned as distinct but related. The rest of the Gospel teaching will add more information to the distinctions and relationships among them, but already a rudimentary revelation of the Blessed Trinity is being given here by the angel Gabriel. This cooperation of the Most High, his Son, and his Holy Spirit shows a very important aspect of Trinitarian doctrine: whenever God acts outside of himself, all three Persons are acting together. The action of each person distinct from the other two applies only to their life within (*ad intram*) the Trinity, while all activity outside (*ad extram*) the Trinity is done in full unity.

Another aspect of the angel's explanation is the connection of the Holy Spirit as the "power" of the Most High throughout Luke-Acts. After Jesus' baptism, he was full of the Holy Spirit (Lk 4:1), and after his temptations he "returned in the power of the Spirit into Galilee" (Lk 4:14). This statement is the basis for his claim to fulfill the passage from Isaiah (61:1-4) that he read in the Nazareth synagogue. Just before his ascension, Jesus promised the apostles that "you shall receive power when the Holy Spirit has come upon you" (Acts 1:8), also linking the Holy Spirit and power. St. Peter makes this connection in his sermon to Cornelius and his household, saying, "God anointed Jesus of Nazareth with the Holy Spirit and with power" (Acts 10:38). However, here, in Mary's womb, the Holy Spirit will demonstrate the "power of the Most High" in a creative act of conceiving a child without the contribution of a man's seed. He will use Mary's ovum but create the rest of Jesus' DNA within her. As such, this will be the one child in all of human history who is the woman's "seed" of Genesis

3:15 that the Lord God had said would arise to strike at the serpent's head and carry on the enmity with the serpent's seed. Gabriel's explanation shows how the fulfillment of the Lord's curse of the serpent becomes possible — for once, a woman truly has seed.

CONSIDER

Another issue surrounding the Annunciation is the use of two verbs to describe the action of the Holy Spirit with Mary: the Holy Spirit "will come upon you" and "overshadow you" (Lk 1:35). At this point, we can connect the presence of the Holy Spirit "overshadowing" Mary with a use of the same Greek verb as used in Exodus.

 Stop here and read **Exodus 40:34-35** in your own Bible.

The Greek verb translated in Exodus as "abode" is the same word used in Luke 1:35 as "overshadow," thereby connecting the cloud of the "glory of the Lord" with the overshadowing Holy Spirit. While the overshadowing in Exodus simply indicated God's presence in the newly completed tent of meeting, the overshadowing of Mary is far

OUR LADY OF THE ARK OF THE COVENANT

The comparison of the overshadowing of the Lord's glory at the tent of meeting with the overshadowing of the Holy Spirit at the Incarnation has led to Mary's title "Ark of the New Covenant." Jesus personifies the New Covenant, which will be in his blood — blood that began to be formed while he took flesh in Mary's womb. Mary is the ark that carries him, and this will evoke John the Baptist's leaping in his mother's womb. Today, a church called Our Lady of the Ark of the Covenant stands over the ancient threshing floor at Kiriath-jearim, where the Ark of the Covenant remained after its return from the Philistines, commemorating this link between the Old and New Testaments.

more creative — God the Son will be conceived in her womb. This is more akin to the "hovering" of the Spirit of God over the chaotic abyss before God spoke in order to create light and everything else.

After announcing that the Holy Spirit will overshadow Mary in order to conceive the child, Gabriel explains that this is the reason he "will be called holy, the Son of God" (Lk 1:35). Holiness will belong to his very nature because he is the Son of God, and therefore he is the "Holy One of Israel." Later in the Gospels, the apostles will worship him after he walks on the water, and they will proclaim, "Truly you are the Son of God" (Mt 14:33). John the Baptist will call him "the Son of God" (Jn 1:34), as will Nathanael (Jn 1:49). And after the Resurrection, Thomas will profess, "My Lord and my God" (Jn 20:28). At this point, Mary takes this message on faith by saying, "Let it be" (Lk 1:38). Her answer is a double acceptance of her own smallness as the "handmaid of the Lord" and of the angel's word as something to be trusted.

FIAT

Mary's answer, "Let it be," requires three English words, but in St. Jerome's Latin only one word is necessary: *Fiat*. The Syriac also uses only one word, *nehweh*, to convey this idea. This one-word acceptance of God's invitation to take a key role in the history of human salvation becomes a model of obedient faith down through the ages.

"Embracing God's salvific will with a full heart and impeded by no sin, she devoted herself totally as a handmaid of the Lord to the person and work of her Son, under Him and with Him, by the grace of almighty God, serving the mystery of redemption. Rightly therefore the holy Fathers see her as used by God not merely in a passive way, but as freely cooperating in the work of human salvation through faith and obedience. For, as St. Irenaeus says, she 'being obedient, became the cause of salvation for herself and for the whole human race.' "

— *Lumen Gentium* (n. 56)

Mary's answer to Gabriel is another link to her as the New Eve. As *Lumen Gentium* (n. 56) brings out: "Hence not a few of the early Fathers gladly assert [with St. Irenaeus] in their preaching, 'The knot of Eve's disobedience was untied by Mary's obedience; what the virgin Eve bound through her unbelief, the Virgin Mary loosened by her faith,' " adding: "The Father of mercies willed that the incarnation should be preceded by the acceptance of her who was predestined to be the mother of His Son, so that just as a woman contributed to death, so also a woman should contribute to life."

MARY AND THE CHURCH FATHERS

Two of the Fathers cited in *Lumen Gentium* who link Mary with Eve belong to the second century. The first is St. Justin Martyr, who debated a Jewish scholar in Ephesus named Trypho. This debate was written down by a witness and is known as *The Dialogue With Trypho*.

The second is St. Irenaeus, the bishop of Lyons, writing in his *Contra Haereses*, Book 3.XXII.4.

Mary is a model for the whole Church and for each of its members. Each person needs the Holy Spirit to overshadow his or her life, since the Holy Spirit makes it possible for people to do what is impossible for mere humans. In that way, we, too, can cooperate with God in undoing the effects of our own sins and those of other people in our society.

DISCUSS

1. What does it mean to you that the angel addressed Mary as "full of grace"? Why was it essential that Mary be "full of grace" if she was to be the mother of the Messiah?

2. The angel Gabriel said that nothing is impossible with God. What evidence of this have you experienced in your own life?

3. What are some of the ways that Mary can be considered the New Eve? Why is important to have a "New Eve"?

PRACTICE

This week, think about one or two areas in your life where God may be calling you to say, *"Fiat* — Let it be!" Pray for wisdom, clarity, and guidance, as well as the courage to surrender your will and your life to God, as Mary did, remembering that by the power of the Holy Spirit, "nothing will be impossible" with God (Lk 1:37).

Session 3

THE VISITATION TO ELIZABETH AND THE ANNUNCIATION TO JOSEPH

"Dear brothers and sisters, our meditation on the human and spiritual journey of St. Joseph invites us to ponder his vocation in all its richness, and to see him as a constant model for all those who have devoted their lives to Christ in the priesthood, in the consecrated life, or in the different forms of lay engagement. Joseph was caught up at every moment by the mystery of the Incarnation. Not only physically, but in his heart as well, Joseph reveals to us the secret of a humanity which dwells in the presence of mystery and is open to that mystery at every moment of everyday life. In Joseph, faith is not separated from action. His faith had a decisive effect on his actions. Paradoxically, it was by acting, by carrying out his responsibilities, that he stepped aside and left God free to act, placing no obstacles in his way. Joseph is a 'just man' (Mt 1:19) because his existence is 'ad-justed' to the word of God."

— Pope Benedict XVI, Address (March 18, 2009)

The Visitation of Mary to Elizabeth can be divided into two parts: the narrative of Mary's visitation to Elizabeth (Lk 1:39-45) and Mary's Canticle, the Magnificat (Lk 1:46-55). In some ways it is a dialogue: in the first part, Elizabeth does all the speaking; in the second, only Mary speaks. However, it is key to note that both women are filled with the Holy Spirit, who inspires their words. As such, their words need to be attended carefully.

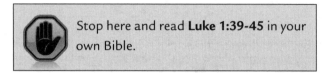
Stop here and read **Luke 1:39-45** in your own Bible.

The setting of the scene is Mary's journey from Nazareth of Galilee to an unnamed city of the Judean hill country; later tradition will identify the town as Ain Karem. The Church of the Visitation is on a hill across a valley from the town, in keeping with the words of Luke 1:24 that Elizabeth "hid herself."

Mary's journey begins immediately after her "Fiat" and is her response to that act of faith: she begins a journey of faith that will take her along many surprising and at times extremely painful travels.

CONSIDER

Pope St. John Paul II compares Mary's Fiat to Abraham's act of faith in responding to the Lord's call to start a new people with a covenant with God. Another aspect of this comparison is that just as Abraham left Haran (in what is now southeast Turkey) to dwell in Canaan as a living out of his faith, so too does Mary take a journey after having heard from the angel Gabriel that Elizabeth was already with child. This is more than an act of faith in the angel's word; it is the beginning of a lifelong journey of faith that will bring her to Bethlehem, Jerusalem, Egypt, Nazareth again, and ultimately to Mount Calvary and finally to the Mount of Olives for the ascension of Jesus. Everyone does well to remember that faith does not remove all the troubles of life, but it guides us on the hard journey of life to accomplish God's will. Faith holds us up through the times when the evidence seems so contrary to our faith. Faith is the reason to rejoice when we see the Lord accomplish deeper truth than we first expected at the start of our journey. The various Marian texts we will study will demonstrate Mary's journey of faith so that we can find strength and support from her as we make our own journey of faith.

STUDY

Elizabeth and the unborn John the Baptist react to Mary's presence, but they do so under the influence of the same Holy Spirit who had overshadowed Mary in order to conceive Jesus within her womb. We read the "babe leaped in her [Elizabeth's] womb" (Lk 1:41). The term for "leap" often refers to sheep, which spring up, all four legs off the ground, when they are excited. The infant John leaps at the presence of the Lord, as prophesied would happen before the "sun of righteousness," an image for the Messiah. Elizabeth then pronounces two beatitudes directed to Mary and her son in her womb: "Blessed are you among women, and blessed is the fruit of your womb!" (Lk 1:42).

Because of its inclusion in the Hail Mary, one of the most frequently repeated verses of Scripture is "Blessed are you among women, and blessed is the fruit of your womb!" The expression "Blessed are you among women" is not good Greek grammar but is good Aramaic grammar, and that opens up an insight into its meaning. Aramaic, Hebrew, and other ancient Semitic languages do not have comparative or superlative forms for adjectives. For instance, in English we usually add "-er" for the comparative and "-est" for the superlative: for example, high, higher, highest. Semitic languages commonly use prepositions to communicate this concept: "more blessed" would be expressed as "you are blessed from him/her/them"; "most blessed" is translated as "blessed among them," as in this verse.

When the Holy Spirit inspires Elizabeth to speak these words, we must take them very seriously. If Mary is "blessed among women," the Aramaic idiom means that she is the "most blessed woman." One can then reflect that since she is the most blessed woman, she is even more blessed than our common mother, Eve, who came into existence without original sin but later fell into it. Mary is more blessed than Eve because Mary was conceived without original sin but never fell into any sin. In this verse, we can see a scriptural basis for Mary's Immaculate Conception.

HOW DID THE NAME "JESUS" GET ADDED TO THE HAIL MARY?

St. Bernardine of Siena, who worked tirelessly to spread devotion to the holy Name of Jesus, was responsible for adding the name "Jesus" to this line of the Hail Mary. He traveled around Italy and other countries with banners bearing the holy Name of Jesus. By adding the Name of Jesus to the Hail Mary ("blessed is the fruit of thy womb, Jesus"), he reminds us that our love of the Blessed Virgin Mary can never be separated from our love of Blessed Jesus.

Elizabeth recognizes that the approach of Blessed Mary is a gift from God, partly signaled by the leaping of her child in her womb, but mostly by the gift of the Holy Spirit coming upon her with inspired words. She acknowledges that "the mother of my Lord" (Lk 1:43) has come to her. She honors Mary, whom she has just proclaimed "blessed," but especially honors Mary's son as her "Lord." This is particularly amazing since Mary had not yet begun to show that she was with child (the trip from Nazareth to the Judean hill country took only three or four days), nor had she yet told Elizabeth anything about it. This act of faith in the presence of her Lord is a supernatural gift of faith. Hence, St. John Paul II wrote in *Redemptoris Mater* (n. 13), "Mary of Nazareth presents herself at the threshold of Elizabeth and Zechariah's house as the Mother of the Son of God. This is Elizabeth's joyful discovery: 'The mother of my Lord comes to me'!" From this, the reader can also recognize that welcoming Mary is at the same time an acceptance and a commitment to her son, Jesus Christ, as Lord.

Elizabeth's third beatitude is directed to Mary because she "believed that there would be a fulfillment of what was spoken to her from the Lord" (Lk 1:45). This, too, is a proclamation inspired by the Holy Spirit, rather than a conclusion drawn from anything Mary had already spoken to her. In *Redemptoris Mater* (n. 12), St. John Paul II wrote that these words have "fundamental importance" because they "can be linked with the title 'full of grace' of the angel's greeting." They "reveal an essential Mariological content, namely the truth about Mary, who has become really present in the mystery of Christ precisely because she 'has believed.' The fullness of grace announced by the angel means the gift of God himself. Mary's faith, proclaimed by Elizabeth at the Visitation, indicates how the Virgin of Nazareth responded to this gift."

Of course, Elizabeth's beatitude of Mary's faith can be directly related to the dialogue between a woman in the crowd and Jesus, during the public ministry, when the woman raised her voice and said to him, "Blessed is the womb that bore you, and the breasts that you sucked!" And he replied, "Blessed rather are those who hear the word of God and keep it!" (Lk 11:27-28).

The words of the woman and the words of Jesus are not mutually exclusive, as Elizabeth's beatitude shows. Mary is blessed both because she conceived Jesus in her womb but even more because she had faith and kept the word of God in her heart.

STUDY

After Elizabeth's Spirit-directed words, Mary now speaks. While Elizabeth has spoken her words to and about Mary and her child, Mary now turns the attention to God our Lord and the various things he is doing and will do for Mary, for the poor and needy, for the proud and wealthy, and for Israel.

Mary's Canticle begins proclaiming her decision to praise God for all that the Lord has done for her, employing many Old Testament expressions and allusions throughout.

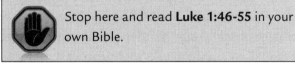

Stop here and read **Luke 1:46-55** in your own Bible.

The opening line uses parallelism between the soul and the spirit. No particular distinction is intended between soul and spirit, but both are parallel ways for Mary to express her inner life being engaged in praising God. Her announcement that she will "magnify" the Lord reflects Psalm 34:3: "O magnify the LORD with me, and let us exalt his name together!" The combining of "magnify" and "rejoice" is found only in Psalm 40:16: "[M]ay all who seek you rejoice and be glad in you; may those who love your salvation say continually, 'Great is the LORD!' " (RSV-SCE).

<table>
<tr><td>

PARALLEL EXPRESSIONS IN THE MAGNIFICAT

The use of parallelism between the phrases as a way to clarify an intended meaning is a typical device of Hebrew poetry. It serves better for a literature destined for international use than does alliteration, rhyming, and other similar devices, since those poetic flourishes cannot be translated into another language but parallel ideas can.

</td></tr>
</table>

Some people have suggested that by calling God "my Savior," Mary is admitting that she is a sinner in need of a Savior. Obviously, she needs God to be her Savior, as all humans do. However, this does not imply that she has committed any sin. One can be saved from quicksand by being pulled out of it after having been trapped in it; one can also be saved from quicksand by being prevented from falling into it in the first place. After the fall of Eve and Adam into sin, the human race is saved by being pulled out of the quicksand of sin that would swallow each person whole if left to his or her own power. Mary, "the one who has been graced" and "the most blessed of women," was saved by being prevented from falling into sin.

I will never forget a radio sermon by a preacher who yelled with force and insistence that Jesus' mother was a sinner in need of a Savior. Had he yelled so emphatically to a broadcast audience that my mother was a sinner in order to make sure everyone accepted that fact, I might have some words with him. I cannot imagine that our Lord Jesus will have found it any more pleasing to hear in regard to his own mother.

Mary then goes on to talk of her "low estate." The Greek word translated as "low estate" means "lowliness, affliction." It is also used in Acts 8:33: "In his humiliation justice was denied him," which quotes Isaiah 53:8: "By oppression and judgment he was taken away," where the Greek Old Testament uses the same word too. In Acts, the affliction and lowliness refers to the suffering of Jesus Christ; here Mary applies the term to her condition as a member of the whole people of Israel that is suffering in a world of sin, grief, and oppression.

"[H]enceforth all generations will call me blessed" (Lk 1:48) is a phrase that picks up from the beatitudes given to Mary by Elizabeth and extends into the future, until the end of the world, that she will be called "blessed." Keep in mind her awareness of her own lowliness as she states this. It is logical to conclude that just as Elizabeth blessed Mary because the Son of God had been conceived in her womb, so will all generations bless her for the same reason. In fact, the very reason she gives for this future designation is that "he who is mighty has done great things for me" (Lk 1:49). This verse explains the common title "Blessed Virgin Mary" being addressed to her throughout the history of the Church, as well as the frequent recitation of the Hail Mary, as a way to live out her prediction for all generations.

> "Hence after the Synod of Ephesus the cult of the people of God toward Mary wonderfully increased in veneration and love, in invocation and imitation, according to her own prophetic words: 'All generations shall call me blessed, because He that is mighty hath done great things to me' (Lk 1:48-49). This cult, as it always existed, although it is altogether singular, differs essentially from the cult of adoration which is offered to the Incarnate Word, as well to the Father and the Holy Spirit, and it is most favorable to it."
>
> — *Lumen Gentium* (n. 66)

Mary then continues, "for he who is mighty has done great things for me, and holy is his name." Here the word "mighty" is *dunatos*, a term meaning "one who is able." This connects with the angel Gabriel's words, "For with God nothing will be impossible" (Lk 1:37). "Impossible" is *adunatesei*, a verbal form of the same root. Her declaration of God as the "mighty one" capable of doing "great things for me" is an example of her beatitude for believing all that the Lord had told her through the angel. Mary clearly recognizes holiness as a quality that belongs to the Lord by his very nature, while her own blessedness is a gift bestowed upon her by the Lord, whether through her faith in his words or through the presence of his Son in her womb.

CONSIDER

Next Mary turns to a description of the Lord's future mercy, with a particular focus on what he will do *to* the proud and mighty and *for* the humble and needy. In addition to the future generations calling her blessed, they will also find his mercy for two reasons. On the one hand, the child she is bearing is the "Son of the Most High; and the Lord God will give to him the throne of his father David, and he will reign over the house of Jacob for ever; and of his kingdom there will be no end" (Lk 1:32-33). His eternal reign will be the source of the mercy that Mary, his mother, announces will last "from generation to generation" (Lk 1:50).

On the other hand, the mercy is available to those "who fear him" (Lk 1:50). Modern culture does not find fear very appealing as a necessary virtue for anything, including the reception of God's mercy. However, Mary's statement of fear as a condition for receiving God's mercy is in line with the Old Testament as well as God's norms for those who find mercy at the end of the world.

INVESTIGATE

 Look up the following passages and make notes on God and his mercy:

PASSAGE	NOTES
Exodus 34:6-7	
Psalm 31:19	
Psalm 85:9	
Psalm 103:11	

Psalm 103:17	
Psalm 115:12-13	
Psalm 118:4	
Revelation 19:5	

STUDY

The claim that the Lord has "scattered the proud" (Lk 1:51) is another common theme in the Old Testament, from which the Magnificat draws. Pride makes faith unlikely if not impossible. The way that the Lord typically deals with the proud is to cause them a harm that helps them realize their smallness and the complete lack of a basis for being proud.

INVESTIGATE

SCATTERING THE PROUD

 Look up the following passages and make notes on how the Lord deals with pride:

PASSAGE	NOTES
1 Samuel 2:3-10	
Psalm 33:10-11	
Isaiah 10:12-13	
Jeremiah 48:29-30	

This part of the Magnificat links social morality and personal morality with the history of salvation that Mary has experienced in her own life and with the history of Israel's. The importance of including this social morality within Mary's hymn shows that the spiritual life cannot be divorced from the moral life. Spirituality, moral living, and the history of salvation for the people of Israel and for individuals need to be integrated into a whole way of life. Mary does that in her hymn in order to point this way of life out to every Christian.

St. Irenaeus explains one aspect of the importance of the Magnificat by pointing out that Mary speaks for the whole Church by connecting the salvation accomplished within her through the incarnation of God's Son to the Old Testament roots of God's promises made to Israel:

> Mary, exulting because of this, cried out, prophesying on behalf of the Church, "My soul doth magnify the Lord, and my spirit has rejoiced in God my Savior. For he has taken up his child Israel, in remembrance of his mercy, as he spoke to our fathers, Abraham, and his seed for ever." By these and such like [passages] the Gospel points out that it was God who spoke to the fathers; that it was he who, by Moses, instituted the legal dispensation, by which giving of the law we know that he spoke to the fathers.

UNDERLYING PUNS

One bit of evidence that a Semitic language original underlies Luke's Greek text is that Hebrew/Aramaic puns appear with the name Elizabeth in the Magnificat and Zechariah in the Benedictus. In Luke 1:53 "he [God] has filled" is a pun on *Elishaba'* ("Elizabeth" in Hebrew), which means "God will satisfy." In the Benedictus (Lk 1:72), Zechariah says the Lord will "remember his holy covenant"; "Zechariah" means "the Lord remembered." These puns do not work in Greek.

One can assume that life returned to its normal rhythm as Mary spent the next three months with Elizabeth — about the time of the remainder of Elizabeth's pregnancy — before returning home to Nazareth.

STUDY

One other piece of Scripture relating to Mary and her pregnancy is the annunciation to Joseph. Unlike the Annunciation narrative in Luke, which centers on the Virgin Mary, Matthew's narrative centers on Joseph, with a short, though important, mention of Mary.

 Stop here and read **Matthew 1:18-25** in your own Bible.

Matthew begins by focusing on the announcement of the baby's conception to Joseph. As in Luke, Mary is described as being betrothed to Joseph, before the two had come together. No description of her part in the process is described, but rather the emphasis is on Joseph's discovery of her being with child. The reader is told that the conception is of the Holy Spirit, but no one else knows yet. A dilemma exists because Joseph knows he is not the father, he does not know who is, yet he is a righteous man who does not want to shame Mary. The latter issue is very important in the Middle East, where shame and honor are important ends of the moral spectrum — they did not live in a world of reality TV or talk shows, where shame is virtually unknown. Joseph's resolve is to divorce her quietly and not add shame to her apparent predicament. Still, nothing is said here about Mary's reaction to his decision.

The resolution is made by God, who sends an angel to Joseph's dream. Clearly, the Lord wants Joseph to take Mary as his wife. He explains that Mary's child was conceived by the Holy Spirit, and that no other man committed adultery with her. The more important fact is that the child is a son, whom Joseph must name Jesus (just as Mary was told in Luke 1:31). The importance of the name comes from its meaning in the Hebrew root *yasha'* ("to save"). His name points to his mission to "save his people from their sins" (Mt 1:21). This message will suffice to make Joseph change his mind about divorcing Mary.

Matthew then comes on to make his own comment on the situation. As is frequent in his Gospel, Matthew mentions that the events taking place are in fact the fulfillment of an Old Testament prophecy. Matthew cites Isaiah 7:14, the sign that Isaiah had said the Lord would give to the fearful King Ahab. As discussed in Session One, the word describing Immanuel's mother as *almah* can mean a young woman. However, here Matthew has the term *parthenos*, specifically meaning "virgin," because he is citing the Greek Old Testament. This makes clear his teaching that Mary conceived her Son virginally, without the influence of any man. Matthew's point in quoting Isaiah is to show that this miraculous anomaly was not simply an unusual occurrence but inherently part of God's long-term plan of salvation, as shown in the prophecy offered 730 years before the event.

This episode concludes with a short narrative statement about Joseph waking from his dream and doing all that the angel of the Lord had commanded him. One slightly controversial point is the statement that Joseph did not know Mary "until she had borne a son" (Mt 1:25). Some try to conclude that since he did not know her "until" she bore her son, he did "know her" after she bore the son, living a normal marital life with her as his wife. Clearly, the point is to confirm the angel's word that the child was conceived by the Holy Spirit, and that Joseph did not have any part in the conception. Later sessions will go into the issue of Jesus' "brothers," demonstrating that they are the children of Mary's sister (also called Mary) and her husband, Clopas.

Once Joseph came to accept that the child was conceived of the Holy Spirit in Mary's womb, and that Jesus was "God among us," he recognized her womb as a place more sacred than Mount Sinai, where the Lord gave Moses tablets of stone, or the Holy of Holies in the Temple, where the golden Ark of the Covenant was kept. The Son of God, who personifies the New Covenant, dwelt in Mary's womb, consecrating it more than any other space on the face of the earth.

DISCUSS

1. What is most significant to you about Mary's visit to Elizabeth?
2. What are some of the qualities of Joseph that would have made him the ideal foster father for Jesus? How did he exhibit those traits in the way he dealt with Mary's unexpected pregnancy?
3. In what ways does the Magnificat demonstrate Mary's profound humility?

PRACTICE

This week, pray the Magnificat and consider how Mary's words relate back to the Old Testament. Reread some of the psalms listed in this section and ask God for his merciful forgiveness of your sins.

Session 4

THE BIRTH AND INFANCY OF JESUS

> "This union of the mother with the Son in the work of salvation is made manifest ... also at the birth of Our Lord, who did not diminish his mother's virginal integrity but sanctified it, when the Mother of God joyfully showed her firstborn son to the shepherds and the Magi."
>
> — *Lumen Gentium* (n. 57)

Luke presents the birth of Jesus most simply, stating that Mary "gave birth to her first-born son" (Lk 2:7). The details of the birth are of less interest than the details that set the birth in historical context and describe its effects on others, so Luke accomplishes an important task in setting the birth of Jesus within the secular history that was known to the rest of the people of the first century. In so doing, he emphasizes that Jesus' birth did not take place in some far distant mythological time but within a real political situation. Luke will do this again when John the Baptist begins his public ministry, which is also the setting for the start of Jesus' public ministry some thirty years after the birth of Jesus.

 Stop here and read **Luke 2:1-20** in your own Bible.

Luke gives the time context as the days when Caesar Augustus was emperor and Quirinius was governor of Syria. It helps to have a little historical background here. Octavian (b. 63 B.C.), an adopted son of Julius Caesar, defeated Caesar's assassins (Brutus and Cassius) in 42 B.C., with the help of Marc Antony. When Marc Antony and Cleopatra went to war against Octavian in 33 B.C., he defeated them three years later, and the Senate in Rome made him *princeps* (chief citizen) and declared him Caesar Augustus in 27 B.C. With the help of his wife Livia, he gained more power, and his reign began the famous *Pax Romana*, a period virtually without war. Quirinius was a very important figure during the reign of Caesar Augustus, having served as governor of Crete and Cyrene, a consul in Rome, governor of Pamphylia/Galatia, and governor of Syria. Later, St. Paul will write in Galatians 4:4 that "when the time had fully come, God sent forth his Son, born of woman," indicating that this *Pax Romana* was a good time for the Messiah to come.

Luke mentions a census as the occasion that induces Joseph to travel the approximately seventy-five miles from Nazareth in Galilee to Bethlehem in Judea. He says that Joseph is of David's family, which means that the child would legally be considered a member of David's lineage and thereby a candidate to be the Messiah promised to David in 2 Samuel 7:11-16. The angel Gabriel had told Mary that "the Lord God will give to him the throne of his father David" (Lk 1:32), indicating her Davidic heritage would be the natural source of Jesus' Davidic heritage.

In addition, Bethlehem is not only the city of David, but it is also mentioned in Micah as the place in which the Messiah would be born.

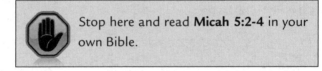 Stop here and read **Micah 5:2-4** in your own Bible.

STUDY

This fulfillment of prophecy remains implied for all who know the Old Testament. Joseph's motive of obeying the rules of enrollment in the census under Roman rule helps emphasize that the fulfillment of the prophecy came through the forces of external, gentile government rather than Joseph and Mary trying to engineer a fulfillment on their own initiative. This pattern will recur on other occasions, as when the Roman soldiers cast lots for Jesus' garment and unwittingly fulfill Psalm 22:18: "[T]hey divide my garments among them, and for my raiment they cast lots."

ROMAN SUBJECTS

A complex point about Roman taxation should be made. Luke is frequently eager to show that the early Christians were good and loyal subjects of Rome. In Luke's second chapter, Joseph readily registers to pay his taxes; much later, Jesus is crucified through false allegations, without having committed any treason; and St. Paul is a good Roman citizen during his trials, especially from his arrest in Jerusalem until his house arrest in Rome. At the same time, modern readers do well to remember that Roman taxes were extremely burdensome, especially to people in the provinces. For that reason, the Zealot party of Jews frequently, and unsuccessfully, revolted against Rome.

At this point, Joseph still is "betrothed" to Mary, which is Luke's way of emphasizing that Jesus is not Joseph's natural child. This connects to the angel Gabriel's words that he "will be called the Son of the Most High" (Lk 1:32). The birth of Jesus is described very simply: "And she gave birth to her first-born son and wrapped him in swaddling cloths, and laid him in a manger, because there was no place for them in the inn" (Lk 2:7).

While swaddling clothes would have been normal for a newborn child, laying him in a manger was not. "Manger," a fourteenth-century word derived from the Old French word for "eat," is a term for an animal's feeding trough. This term is the basis for understanding that Jesus was born in a stable, which is the normal place to find a manger.

(Incidentally, this chapter is a demonstration of the only mention of Jesus' mother in St. Paul's writings: "But when the time had fully come, God sent forth his Son, born of woman, born under the law" [Gal 4:4].)

CHURCH OF THE NATIVITY IN BETHLEHEM

Early Christians visited a cave in the center of Bethlehem where they believed Jesus had been born. However, to prevent the Christians from going there, Emperor Hadrian built a temple to Adonis over the site around the year 135. When St. Helena came to the Holy Land in 325, the local Christians pointed to Hadrian's temple as the place of the birth. She ordered it torn down and found a cave below it, with two mangers still inside. One manger was sent to Rome and the other remains in the cave to this day. Then she built a church there. When the Samaritans burned that church, Byzantine Emperor Justinian built a new one in the sixth century, which still stands for Christians to visit on pilgrimage.

WHY WE CELEBRATE CHRISTMAS ON DECEMBER 25

No one can be sure of the precise date of Christmas. However, Christians began celebrating two different dates — December 25 and January 6 — by the late second or early third century. The basis of these dates came from traditions concerning the date of the crucifixion — March 25 in the West and April 6 in the Eastern churches. They linked Jesus' saving death with his birth by dating Christmas nine months after the day of Jesus' death — December 25 or January 6. Some people have linked December 25 to the Roman celebration of Sol Invictus, the "Unconquered Sun." However, it was Emperor Aurelian who instituted this celebration by dedicating the Temple of Sol Invictus on December 25, in the year 276, years after Christians had already celebrated the day as Christ's birth date.

STUDY

After the birth itself, Luke continues the account with an ordinary situation of the region — shepherds keeping guard of their sheep. Even today, panthers and jackals roam the Judean hills. In ancient times, lions, wolves, and bears also posed a threat. However, as Luke points out, the shepherds' focus is on the sheep. Then their attention shifts to an angel of the Lord and the Lord's glory, which evoke fear from them, parallel to the priest Zechariah being "troubled" with "fear" and the Virgin Mary being "greatly troubled" at St. Gabriel's approach (Lk 1:12, 29).

As usual, the angel begins with a command not to fear his presence.

Next he announces that he was sent to bring "good news," just as Gabriel had said to Zechariah: "I was sent to speak to you, and to bring you this good news" (Lk 1:19). However, the message to these humble shepherds in the fields is greater than the message to Zechariah in the Temple: a Savior, Christ the Lord, is born in nearby Bethlehem.

Lastly, the angel's message includes a sign of seeing the newborn baby in swaddling cloths and lying in a manger, precisely the description that Luke had given the reader earlier. This means that Mary's simple actions within the poverty of having given birth in a stable are now a sign to which the angel of the Lord directs the poor, simple shepherds. In this sense, Mary is taking yet another role in evangelizing others about Jesus, and a heavenly angel describes her action as a sign for the shepherds.

INVESTIGATE

"FEAR NOT" (NO. 2)

 Look up the following passages and make notes on angelic appearances:

PASSAGE	NOTES
Daniel 10:12, 19	
Matthew 28:5	
Luke 1:13	
Luke 1:30	
Revelation 1:17-18	

SHEPHERDS' FIELD

About a mile from the Church of the Nativity in Bethlehem is a chapel of the Shepherds' Field, in the present-day village of Beit Sahour. To protect their sheep from predators at night, shepherds would have had easy access to a number of caves there. Many years of excavation have revealed a first-century baptistery and the ruins of a number of Byzantine-era monasteries (fourth through sixth centuries), plus many artifacts, including presses for making Eucharistic bread. This ancient and venerable tradition of Christian meditation and worship at this site continues with the chapels inside each cave and the Chapel of the Angels built above them.

The scene suddenly changes to a whole host of angels praising God as their response to the announcement of the sign of the birth of Christ the Lord. It is as if heaven cannot restrain itself, and it erupts into adoration. Of course, the Church has taken the words of the angels' canticle as its own, continuing to praise God through the centuries in the Gloria at Mass, with an expansion along the lines of faith in the Blessed Trinity and Jesus' saving role as the Lamb of God.

ANGELS TEACH US HOW TO WORSHIP

Jewish and Christian liturgies have learned proper worship from the hymns of the angels over the millennia. Both communities make use of the Seraphim's hymn in Isaiah 6:3: "Holy, holy, holy is the LORD of hosts; the whole earth is full of his glory." Christians also expand the canticle of the angels into the Gloria at Mass, and many hymns are developed from the praise of the angels and saints in Revelation.

The shepherds respond to the angel's message by an explicit decision to go to Bethlehem to see what the Lord has made known to them. Note that they do not go to see if it is true but to see what has happened. In so deciding, the shepherds demonstrate exemplary faith, and certainly a faith beyond that of Zechariah, who wanted some evidence of Gabriel's message. In Luke 2:16-17, their eagerness to see what has happened is expressed with their "haste," parallel to the Virgin Mary's "haste" to go visit Elizabeth to see what the Lord had done with her kinswoman. These simple men find everything that has been told them by the angel. As shepherds already familiar with the care of animals, they do not need to search the houses door-to-door to find Jesus (but they would have searched the stables for the right manger — the only manger with a baby in it).

When they behold the newborn child, they speak about the message of the angel. People "wondered" (Lk 2:18), a word also translated in other passages as "be amazed at" (*thaumazo*). How else would these shepherds have come to a stable looking for a child unless the angel had revealed it? The angel's description of the child as a "Savior, who is Christ the Lord" (Lk 2:11) would have been astonishing. While Moses' being hidden as an infant and floating in the Nile until rescued by Pharaoh's daughter would provide Jewish hearers a precedent for such humble origins, they would wonder and be amazed by all that the shepherds said.

CONSIDER

Mary observed all these events and pondered them in a wider context of all that God had done with her over the preceding nine months. She "kept" all these things that were happening around her (Lk 2:19). She was concerned to care for her newborn son. However, the appearance of totally unknown shepherds, along with their explanation of having been sent to the stable to see a child in a manger, evoked an unexpected keeping of these events in her heart. The Greek word *suntereo* generally means "protect, defend against harm," but in secular texts it also meant "keep in one's mind, be concerned about something." Here the nuance is "hold, keep, treasure up in one's mind." The data of God's revelation ought to be kept and "treasured" and become a reason for one's concern. In this, Mary provides an important model.

The word "ponder" (*sumballo*) has the word "throw" (*ballo*) as its root, with the prefix "with" (*sun* — "n" changes to "m" before "b" and "p"). The word ranges in meaning from "converse" to "fall in with, engage, or fight someone." This variety of meanings adds nuances to the word "ponder" that include interaction with a new idea and struggling with it. This and other passages show that Mary did not fully understand everything that was happening to her, but she kept them all and sought to sort them out in contemplation. As such, she presents a key model for every Christian's meditation on the truth of the Gospel. We, too, must engage our hearts and minds in contemplating the mysteries of our faith, and engage our minds to integrate and understand them better. Such is the task of Christian life. The whole Church throughout its entire history has been blessed by Mary's pondering these events in her heart and passing them on so that they can be contemplated by everyone ever since. Our meditative prayer may also be of service to other people around us, if we are willing to be engaged by the truth and mystery of God.

This episode concludes with the shepherds returning to their flocks as different men. They are now "glorifying and praising God" for all they have heard from the angel and have seen in the stable (Lk 2:20). They understand the fulfillment of revelation within their personal history and experience, and this gets them to focus on God.

STUDY

Luke then proceeds to talk about the circumcision and the manifestation of Jesus who is "born under the law."

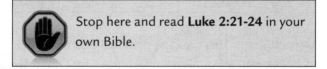

Stop here and read **Luke 2:21-24** in your own Bible.

This passage has a number of rich, and even complicated elements, including parallels with John the Baptist's circumcision and manifestation. However, a key theme will be the fact that Mary and

Joseph obey the Law of Moses and within those circumstances the Holy Spirit will act within people to make Jesus manifest. Unlike the lengthy narrative of the circumcision of John the Baptist in Luke 1:59-80, Jesus' circumcision is described in one verse. His name is given at this ceremony, as happened with John. However, while the naming of John was the center of controversy (Elizabeth and Zechariah wanted to name him John as St. Gabriel had instructed them, while the relatives had their own ideas), the naming of Jesus is simply accomplished in accord with the name the angel had given him.

The commandment to circumcise boy babies on the eighth day after their birth was given to Abraham as a sign of an everlasting covenant with the Lord, a covenant that was personal, irreversible, and hidden — qualities that the Lord desired as its characteristics. God ordered Abraham to enact this sign at the time when God changed his name from Abram to Abraham. Because circumcision was the occasion of Abram's change of name to Abraham, we see both at Jesus' and at John's circumcision that the name is given to each boy at his circumcision ceremony.

The theme that Jesus is "born under the law" continues with discussions about the ceremonies of the purification of Mary and the presentation of Jesus, both in accord with the Law.

Since Luke mentions that the time for the fulfillment of the Law of Moses had come, we do well to look at the laws. These verses refer to the law of their purification first.

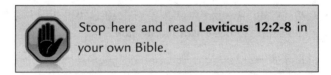

Stop here and read **Leviticus 12:2-8** in your own Bible.

The instructions in this passage primarily concern the mother of a baby and her purification. The underlying ideas stem from Israel's attitude toward the processes of birth and sex. The most off-putting term to modern people is "unclean," since it is also associated in some texts with moral impurity and seems to treat normal sexual processes as "dirty." Such modern concerns miss the point of Israelite teachings.

A better starting point is that God is the author of life, and therefore all the processes of life belong to him as a sacred realm. Moderns see sexuality in a secular way that is commonly divorced from God (unless someone gets married in church, and even that is a very casual issue). However, since Israel knew that God was the source of life, all the processes of human reproduction belonged to him and were, in a certain sense, sacred.

Another difficult concept for moderns is that in the Israelite religion sacred things can make anyone who touches them unclean. This was so true of Mount Sinai that anyone — man or beast — who touched the mountain would be killed for profaning the sacred place where God spoke to Moses. Up to the present day, Jews are forbidden to touch a handwritten Torah scroll (this does not apply to printed Bibles). Touching the sacred text makes the person "unclean," and he must go to the ritual bath (a *mikveh*) to wash off the sacredness.

A similar principle applies to the process of human sexual reproduction — menstruation, a man's nocturnal emission, or childbirth. These belong to God's realm because he is the author of life, and therefore these are sacred to him. It is for that reason that sexual reproductive processes make persons unclean. It has nothing to do with sex being dirty, sinful, or any such concept. Since the Virgin Mary had entered this sacred realm whereby God gives life, she, too, had to go through the process of ritual purification after the birth of her son.

CONSIDER

Next Luke mentions the law of the firstborn who opens the womb. The Old Testament background goes back to Exodus, to the point where the Lord is preparing Israel for the tenth plague against Egypt: the death of the firstborn. In addition to the rules for the Passover lamb and meal, the rules for the future concern the attitude Israel should have toward the imminent death of the Egyptian firstborn sons. They are not to gloat over the pain others will suffer so they can be free. Rather, the rules for the sacrifices for Israelite firstborn sons and domestic animals will always remind them of the suffering of the Egyptians.

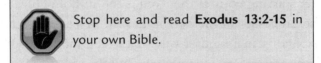

Stop here and read **Exodus 13:2-15** in your own Bible.

This law is not concerned with the processes of nature and the purification of the mother but with the history of Israel's salvation. Israel was saved from slavery, and the Egyptians' attempt to exterminate Israel by killing all the sons as soon as they were born fails. One of the boys to escape the slaughter, Moses, is chosen by God to lead Israel out of Egypt. A series of punishing plagues builds up the crescendo of warning to Egypt, but at each turn Pharaoh fails to let Israel leave, at least until the last plague. In that final punishment, all the firstborn sons die in Egypt, including Pharaoh's son. This punishment fit the crime of the Egyptians having killed the Israelite boys, since the Lord considered Israel his firstborn.

Still, after the plague strikes Egypt on the first Passover, Israel does not gloat, as seen in the reserved description of the effects of the plague and in accepting the law of the dedication of their own firstborn sons and animals. Of course, the Lord forbade human sacrifice, so a substitutionary sacrifice of a lamb was to be offered. However, the dedication of the firstborn was so important that the Law allowed the poor to offer easily available doves or pigeons as a substitute for the boys. Luke mentions the doves and pigeons to indicate the relative poverty of the Holy Family.

Luke thus shows that Joseph and Mary are eager to live out the laws, thereby exhibiting St. Paul's point about Christ being born "under the law." However, as the nature of these laws indicates, God is Lord over both the processes of nature, including human reproduction in all its aspects, and the history of salvation. This helps demonstrate the two foci of God's relation to everyone in the world: he is the Creator and the Redeemer. These are the points around which most of Sacred Scripture revolves, and this applies to Jesus Christ as well.

STUDY

Luke's attention now shifts from the concern to obey the Law to the presence of a devout and righteous man named Simeon, who was directed by the Holy Spirit to encounter the infant Jesus and his mother, Mary.

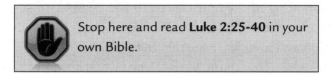

Stop here and read **Luke 2:25-40** in your own Bible.

This section begins with a description of Simeon's character as a way to introduce the role of the Holy Spirit. He is described as "righteous and devout" (Lk 2:25), a description similar to that of other people in Scripture, such as Noah, Job, Daniel, Zechariah, and Elizabeth, all of whom were advanced in years yet did not use their lifetime to commit evil.

One does well to reflect on the way the Lord uses such righteous, blameless, and devout individuals in his plans, not because they have earned his grace through their righteousness but because such people are willing to cooperate with the Lord. Their moral integrity makes them capable of becoming the Lord's instruments, particularly since most of them are invited to partake of difficult tasks in the salvation of the human race: Noah survives the flood, Job is attacked by Satan, and Daniel is in the lions' den.

One of the most interesting elements of this section is that while Joseph and Mary simply come to the Temple during the process of obeying the Law of the Lord, the Holy Spirit leads this "righteous and devout" old man Simeon to encounter them. This convergence of events shows that obeying the Law does not prevent the action of the Holy Spirit. When we experience a conflict between obeying God's moral law and some other spiritual experience, we would do well to remember humbly how God worked within the Law to bring about the inspiration of his Holy Spirit in the Temple. For example, an individual may feel torn between strong attraction to another person and a commitment to a spouse. However, the person can see that in obedience to the commandment against adultery, the Lord may work very powerfully in him for some purpose he does not yet understand.

Notice, too, that the Holy Spirit had promised that Simeon would see the Messiah before he died. However, there is no evidence that the Holy Spirit told him that this was the day. He simply responded to the prompting of the Spirit to go to the Temple. In so doing, he meets the Messiah in the arms of a couple completing their duties of purification and a sacrifice for the firstborn.

Upon seeing the infant Jesus, Simeon takes him into his arms and proclaims the following short canticle: "Lord, now let your servant depart in peace, according to your word; for my eyes have seen your salvation which you have prepared in the presence of all peoples, a light for revelation to the Gentiles, and for glory to your people Israel" (Lk 2:29-32).

Simeon speaks directly and personally to God: You can let me die in peace because the goal of my life — seeing the Messiah with my own eyes — has occurred. Having received this promise of seeing the Messiah, Simeon most likely would have had a picture of the Messiah in his mind. Based on the descriptions of the Messiah as a conquering king, he might well have expected to see a victorious conqueror coming to take the throne of David. Humans commonly imagine the implementation of their hopes and dreams. What is amazing is that Simeon displays no sign of disappointment at seeing only a six-week-old child of two poor parents. Rather, he "blessed God" (Lk 2:28) for what he did see and proclaimed a canticle that continues to be sung in the Church to this day — the Latin Rite Night Prayer always includes the Canticle of Simeon.

Simeon describes the infant Jesus as God's "salvation" which the Lord had "prepared" over the centuries of Israel's salvation history. Though this preparation had taken place within Israel, it was accomplished in "the presence of all peoples" — that is, within this real world and within its history. This helps explain why Luke included the historical notes at the very start of chapter two, so that the reader can also see Simeon's point about the salvation coming in the sight of all peoples.

CONSIDER

The next part of the chapter has two aspects: Jesus is the "light for revelation to the Gentiles, and for glory to your people Israel" (Lk 2:32 — RSV-SCE). This emphasizes that his birth and the salvation he brings are not just for Israel but also for the whole world. Luke's Gospel will highlight a number of gentiles who witness Jesus as salvation, and his second volume, Acts of the Apostles, will show the history of the Church as it moves from an exclusively Jewish community to an ever increasingly gentile community as well. Simeon's prophetic words help set the theme of these two books of Scripture.

While both father and mother react to Simeon's words and actions, Simeon addresses only Mary. Culturally, it would have been much more expected for an unfamiliar man to address the man of the family. While Simeon does bless both Joseph and Mary, he speaks only to her, and he speaks words that are not easy to hear.

First, he speaks a word about the infant Jesus, whom he is still holding in his arms: Jesus is set, by a destiny beyond the parents' possible expectations, to be "the fall and rising of many in Israel" (Lk 2:34). Just as Simeon's canticle states a major theme of the light of the gentiles and the glory of Israel for Luke's Gospel and Acts, so does this phrase establish a key to reading Luke and Acts. Repeatedly, the reader will observe that some people reject Jesus and others accept him in both of Luke's books, often side by side. Simeon's words highlight one's reading of Luke-Acts, but they apply to the other Gospels as well. In addition, this phrase rings through the centuries as people still reject Jesus and fall, while others accept him and love him, knowing they will rise with him. Inevitably, each person must make the core decision about Jesus and fall from him or rise with him.

Closely related to this is that Jesus is a sign that is spoken against. Pope St. John Paul II said about this phrase that Simeon's words "tell her of the actual historical situation in which the Son is to accomplish his mission, namely, in misunderstanding and sorrow" (*Redemptoris Mater*, n. 16). This point will be clearly seen in the Gospels when Jesus casts out demons and his opponents see it as the power of Satan at work in him, when people reject him, and especially at his trial before the Sanhedrin. Jesus will remain a sign of contradiction when the apostles are put on trial in Jerusalem, when St. Stephen refutes his opponents in debates, when St. Paul begins to preach after his conversion (and throughout his career as an evangelist around the Mediterranean world), and on throughout Christian history into the present age. Again, every person must decide whether Jesus is a sign of hope and love or contradiction.

Lastly, Simeon addresses Mary with a two-part prophecy that contains an extraordinarily hard word for a young, brand-new mother who simply cares about loving her baby like any normal new mother. First he says, "a sword will pierce through your own soul" (Lk 2:35). Since the soul is spiritual and cannot be physically pierced, this is obviously a figure of speech for a profound pain that will enter Mary's life because of her child. Simeon gives no other information, but the danger hangs over her life from that point onward. As St. John Paul II wrote, these words reveal "to her that she will have to live her obedience of faith in suffering, at the side of the suffering Savior, and that her motherhood will be mysterious and sorrowful" (*Redemptoris Mater*, n. 16). Simply hearing such words would have been a cause of great distress for this young woman; she would spend the next years reflecting on what Simeon had told her.

The second phrase explains that this sword will enter Mary so "that thoughts out of many hearts may be revealed" (Lk 2:35). The pain will not be derived from some fault of her own, nor will it occur for her own sake. Rather, her pain will be oriented to the revealing of other people's inner thoughts. Some English translations place the phrase about the sword piercing her soul in parentheses or use some other device to separate those words from this prophecy about revealing the thoughts of many hearts.

No other patriarch, prophet, or saint is said to suffer in order to reveal the inner thoughts of many other people. Mary alone, of all the saints, has been designated as such. This phrase becomes a key to the development of Mariology (the theology of Mary) because of its reference to Mary's distinctive role in revealing inner thoughts. Based on this verse, many people seek out a relationship with Mary in prayer because they want to understand their own inner thoughts. They recognize that her pilgrimage of faith entailed much suffering, and they find a resonance in her pain as they look at Jesus through Mary's eyes. A scene in the movie *The Passion of the Christ* that touched millions was that of Mary seeing Jesus carrying his cross, with her flashbacks to him as a child stumbling. Hardly a parent could hold back tears because the scene awakened their inner thoughts about their own children. Mary's innocent suffering on her pilgrimage of faith is a source of strength to all who struggle and suffer through their lives. It should be no wonder that in light of this verse a whole branch of theology of Mary should arise.

OUR LADY OF THE SEVEN SORROWS

A particular devotion to the Seven Sorrows of Mary arose in the thirteenth century and was promoted by the Servite order, whose spirituality was especially connected to the Seven Sorrows. Feasts of Mary's Seven Sorrows (or the Mater Dolorosa) were celebrated locally and by the Servites, but Pope Pius VII added the feast to the universal calendar in 1814, after the French Revolution and Napoleonic Wars had devastated Europe.

The Seven Sorrows are:

1. Simeon foretells the sword piercing Mary's soul (Lk 2:34-35).
2. The flight into Egypt (Mt 2:13-15).
3. The child Jesus is lost in the Temple (Lk 2:43-50).
4. Mary sees Jesus on the Way of the Cross.
5. The crucifixion and death of Jesus (Jn 19:25-27).
6. Mary receives the body of Jesus in her arms (Mt 27:57-59).
7. The body of Jesus is laid in the tomb (Jn 19:40-42).

The Chaplet of the Seven Sorrows is said by reciting one Our Father and seven Hail Marys while contemplating each Sorrow. Every Sorrow is connected to Jesus and is not about Mary's concerns. All aspects of Mary's importance have to do with Jesus Christ and his mission of the salvation of the world. This connection with Jesus (and insight into him) is the reason we spend so much time meditating on the Mysteries of the Rosary, the Chaplet of the Seven Sorrows, and other aspects of Blessed Mary's life.

STUDY

Before Mary and Joseph leave the Temple, Anna the prophetess comes upon the scene. The description of Anna's life, which is longer than the description of her reaction to seeing the infant Jesus, serves two roles. First, it establishes that she, like Simeon, was a righteous and pious person. She lived a very long widowhood in extraordinary piety — praying and fasting for years — as a preparation through which she was open to recognizing the Messiah when he arrived in the Temple. The text does not state that she had received a promise to see him as Simeon had, but she recognizes him when he appears. Second, the description of her life points to a kind of connection with Simeon's words to Mary about suffering. Anna suffered considerably in her life — involuntarily through widowhood and voluntarily through much fasting and watching in the Temple. Having passed through a long, difficult life, she now rejoices in being in the Messiah's presence. In this, she shows that suffering is not meaningless, but in the light of Christ of which Simeon spoke it acquires a new meaning.

Luke then describes her reaction to the presence of the infant Messiah. She has not yet been introduced to the Holy Family and she does not know the child's name, but she is immediately filled with thanksgiving to God. No mention is made of a subsequent introduction, but Luke immediately moves to her evangelizing efforts to tell about Jesus to everyone who was "looking for the redemption of Jerusalem" (Lk 2:38). No further reference is made about the effect of her announcement. Presumably, this elderly woman died before Jesus' public ministry, and no mention is ever made about anyone who might have heard her announcement and later connected it with Jesus. Yet the description of the people with whom she spoke as those "looking for the redemption of Jerusalem" may indicate a determining characteristic of the persons who later did come to believe in Jesus.

Finally, Luke's conclusion has two foci: the actions of Joseph and Mary and the child Jesus. Joseph and Mary finished all of the rituals required by the Law, again bringing out the theme of Jesus being "born under the Law" from Galatians 4:4. They return to Nazareth in Galilee and to a normal life pursuing the tasks of daily living with no mention of anything extraordinary until Jesus is twelve. As for Jesus, he "grew and became strong" (Lk 2:40), in reference to his physical development. Spiritually, he was filled with wisdom, a quality that the people around him would notice in his manner of speaking and reacting. The "favor" or "grace" of God could not be seen as readily as wisdom in a child, but it is a characteristic he shares with his mother, as shown in the angel Gabriel's greeting to her as "Hail one who has been graced" (or "favored").

DISCUSS

1. What new insights into the Presentation in the Temple did you obtain from this chapter? Why was the Presentation so important to the understanding that Jesus was born "under the law"?

2. What role does the Holy Spirit play in both Simeon's prophecy and Anna's recognition of the Messiah? How can the Holy Spirit help you to recognize Jesus as the Messiah?

3. How does the Jewish understanding of "unclean" — meaning having come in contact with something sacred, of God — give you a new insight into the Immaculate Conception?

PRACTICE

This week, meditate on the Seven Sorrows of Mary. Pray the Chaplet of the Seven Sorrows and consider how Mary's sorrows make her the ideal companion when you are suffering your own sorrow and pain.

Session 5

THE MAGI AND JESUS' CHILDHOOD

> "When the Child Jesus was lost and they had sought Him sorrowing, His parents found Him in the temple, taken up with the things that were His Father's business; and they did not understand the word of their Son. His Mother indeed kept these things to be pondered over in her heart (cf. Lk. 2:41-51)."
>
> — *Lumen Gentium* (n. 57)

For the next part of our study, we move from Luke to Matthew. Much of Matthew's account concerns Christ's infancy, but the material on his early childhood is deeply rooted in the infancy events in a way that makes it logical to look at that part of his childhood as well.

 Stop here and read **Matthew 2:1-18** in your own Bible.

Matthew describes the birth of Jesus with even more restraint than Luke. In his account, the birth has already occurred in Bethlehem at the time of Herod the Great (made king of Judea in 37 B.C. by the Roman general Marc Antony), as the background for introducing the larger drama concerning the Magi.

"Magi" was a term for the Persian priests of Zoroastrian religion, and it referred to magicians (a word derived from "magi"), astrologers, and wise men with secret knowledge. They quickly become the focus of Herod's attention when they ask about the one who is born "king of the Jews" (Mt 2:2), whose star they had seen in the East — the region from which they had come.

JEWS AND THE MAGI

Jews had lived in Babylon since their exile there in 587 B.C., and Jews had spread into the Persian Empire (called the Parthian Empire by the first century and later), as evidenced in books like Tobit. Their widespread presence would have made familiarity with the Jewish people possible for these magi, although the Magi were not familiar with the Jewish Scriptures.

Herod was "troubled" when he heard the Magi's announcement, a reaction that will occur again when Jesus is an adult and comes to Jerusalem riding a donkey. Herod inquires of the "chief priests and scribes," the groups directly parallel to the Magi's position and role, and also the groups that would later oppose Jesus during the public ministry, especially at his trials (Mt 2:3, 4).

At this point, they identify the messianic passage in Micah 5:2 as the way to find the birthplace of the Messiah: "But you, O Bethlehem Ephrathah, who are little to be among the clans of Judah, from you shall come forth for me one who is to be ruler in Israel, whose origin is from of old, from ancient days." What is especially significant in this eighth-century-B.C. prophecy is the mention of the child born in Bethlehem becoming the ruler of Israel, just as the angel Gabriel had said to Mary. One interesting note is that Matthew in the Septuagint version skips the term *Ephrathah*, which was the name of David's clan and apparently not of interest to Matthew and his readers.

Herod then instructs the Magi to find the child in Bethlehem and report to him. At this point, the reader is as naive as the Magi about Herod's evil intents, assuming he wants to worship the child as well. However, the Magi soon come to see the truth of this situation, and after having learned the prophecy about the Messiah's birthplace, they see the star again and follow it with joy. Some have tried to make a positive evaluation of their astrological career, but these astrology apologists forget that the star initially brought the Magi as far as Herod the murderer. Scripture pointed out the rest of the way, and in the context of guidance through God's revelation in Scripture they see the star again.

STUDY

The Magi then enter the house and see the child with Mary, his mother. Note that St. Joseph, who was the main character in Matthew's first chapter, where his genealogy and his dream are narrated, is not mentioned in this scene at all. This is a way for Matthew to emphasize that the child is Mary's, and not Joseph's natural-born son. The Magi worship the child and bring him gifts of gold, frankincense, and myrrh. Their worship is a recognition of the divinity that the angel proclaimed to Joseph in his dream: "[T]hat which is conceived in her is of the Holy Spirit," and "his name shall be called Emmanuel (which means, God with us)" (Mt 1:20, 23).

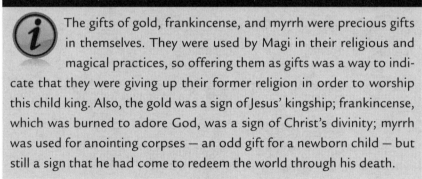

GOLD, FRANKINCENSE, AND MYRRH

The gifts of gold, frankincense, and myrrh were precious gifts in themselves. They were used by Magi in their religious and magical practices, so offering them as gifts was a way to indicate that they were giving up their former religion in order to worship this child king. Also, the gold was a sign of Jesus' kingship; frankincense, which was burned to adore God, was a sign of Christ's divinity; myrrh was used for anointing corpses — an odd gift for a newborn child — but still a sign that he had come to redeem the world through his death.

Finally the Magi learn in a dream at least part of the truth about Herod's evil intents for the child, so they obey the dream rather than King Herod by taking a different route home instead of returning through Jerusalem.

Prior to an explicit mention of Herod's evil intent, the Lord takes the initiative to protect Jesus, his mother, and Joseph by sending his angel to Joseph in yet another dream — his second one so far.

The angel instructs Joseph to flee to Egypt because Herod plans to search for the child to destroy him. Joseph again obeys the dream and takes the child and his mother to Egypt until Herod dies.

The prophecy cited here is Hosea 11:1: "When Israel was a child, I loved him, and out of Egypt I called my son." Hosea referred to the whole people of Israel as the Lord's son, but here Matthew wants the reader to understand that Jesus is the Son of God in a distinctive way.

The difficulty of leaving their homeland for a country they did not know, without job or home, makes this the Blessed Mother's Second Sorrow of the devotion to her Seven Sorrows. An important aspect of this sorrow is that it highlights yet another difficulty in Mary's journey of faith. Being called to be the mother of the Messiah did not entail a life of comfort and ease. Rather, her acceptance of the call meant a difficult life with many challenges. Faith does not make life easy, but it opens a person to the challenges of a lifelong relationship with the mystery of the infinite God, as well as the confrontation with the "mystery of evil."

> "[T]he Son of Mary, and his Mother with him, will experience in themselves the truth of those other words of Simeon: 'a sign that is spoken against' (Lk 2:34). Simeon's words seem like a second Annunciation to Mary, for they tell her of the actual historical situation in which the Son is to accomplish his mission, namely, in misunderstanding and sorrow. While this announcement on the one hand confirms her faith in the accomplishment of the divine promises of salvation, on the other hand it also reveals to her that she will have to live her obedience of faith in suffering, at the side of the suffering Savior, and that her motherhood will be mysterious and sorrowful."
>
> — Pope St. John Paul II, *Redemptoris Mater* (n. 16)

The realization that the Magi had not informed him about the infant king sent Herod into a rage (for which he was famous) that motivated him to order the execution of all baby boys in the region.

This scene brings to mind the rage of the dragon when the woman's child escapes his attempt to devour him (Rev 12:1-17). Despite Herod's efforts to control the events around him, he nonetheless ends up fulfilling a prophecy from Jeremiah 31:15. The "voice in Ramah" and "Rachel weeping for her children" refer to the Bethlehem locale, where Rachel's tomb is located. Rachel had died near Bethlehem while in childbirth (Gen 35:16-20), and the death of these baby boys — now known as the Holy Innocents — is seen by Matthew as the cause of her weeping as prophesied by Jeremiah.

HEROD AND THE HOLY INNOCENTS

The Jewish historian Josephus does not mention the death of the baby boys in Bethlehem, but he lists enough other atrocities by Herod to make this entirely believable. For instance, as Herod was dying he ordered his soldiers to round up a large group of the sons of the Jewish nobility. He knew the people would not mourn his death, so he ordered the execution of the young men in order to give everyone something to mourn about. Fortunately, when he died, the soldiers did not consider his orders valid anymore and they let the young men go free. Ironically, Herod was buried in Herodion, a large fortress on the outskirts of Bethlehem. Archaeologists think they may have discovered his tomb in April-May 2007.

STUDY

In Joseph's third dream, the angel of the Lord instructs Joseph to return to the land of Israel. His orders specifically refer to the child and his mother, whom he is to bring back to Israel. As with his other two dreams, Joseph obeys the message precisely.

 Stop here and read **Matthew 2:19-23** in your own Bible.

The return of Joseph, Mary, and Jesus to Israel does not remove all risk. The new king, Archelaus, could be just as dangerous as his father, Herod. In fact, even the Romans became disgusted with him and deposed him from power in A.D. 6, placing Judea under the governor of Syria, Quirinius, who appointed a procurator to rule the territory — the title later belonging to Pontius Pilate. Therefore, following Joseph's fourth and last dream, the Holy Family journeyed around Judea and settled in the territory of Galilee.

THE ANOMALY OF HEROD'S DEATH

Herod the Great died in 4 B.C., an anomaly since this means that Jesus was born B.C. (Before Christ). This problem comes from a mistake in dating made by Dionysius Exiguus, who had been commissioned by Byzantine Emperor Justinian to determine the date of Christ's birth so that the reference for all dates would switch from the founding of Rome and the Olympiads (the four-year period between Olympic games) to the birth of Jesus Christ. When the emperor hurried his work, Dionysius miscalculated the Olympiad in which Herod died, thereby making a four-year gap between the death of Herod and the year 1 (there is no year zero because the zero had not been invented yet).

The move to Nazareth in Galilee is understood as the fulfillment of a prophecy that cannot be found in the precise form reported in Matthew — "He shall be called a Nazarene" (Mt 2:23) — and this has confused scholars. Greek has only one "z" sound, while Hebrew has two, equivalent to the English "z" and to a "ts" sound. The problem was resolved when an ancient list of the country's towns was discovered, including "Nazareth," the only ancient Hebrew copy of the town's name showing that it used the letter *tsadeh*, which is equivalent to the "ts" sound. The Hebrew word *netzer* is the basis of Nazareth, and it means "shoot" of a tree. Therefore, the messianic prophecy being fulfilled is that Jesus is "[the] shoot from the stump of Jesse" (Is 11:1). This maintains his Davidic background (Jesse was

David's father) and yet explains why he lived in Nazareth, the place of the shoot, in Galilee, so far north of David's city of Bethlehem or his capital city, Jerusalem.

CONSIDER

Many people wonder about the connection between the infancy stories of Jesus in Luke and Matthew. Neither evangelist knows of certain episodes that the other emphasizes. However, neither do the different episodes make the others impossible. Both agree that Mary became pregnant with Jesus while she was betrothed to Joseph, and both teach that she conceived by the Holy Spirit and not by any man, including Joseph. They both agree on Bethlehem as the birthplace and on the name given to the child by the angel. When they have points of fact in common, they agree with each other and confirm each another. However, each highlights a different set of events that the author considered important for his particular readers.

Luke is frequently concerned that his gentile audience understand that neither Jesus nor his followers were seditious against the Roman Empire. Throughout Luke and Acts, he highlights compatibility between imperial concerns and Christian teaching. For that reason, a story that made a client king, such as Herod the Great, look bad would not go over very well. He even de-emphasizes the role of Herod Antipas in the death of John the Baptist, passing over the event fairly simply, in contrast to the other evangelists. Matthew does not highlight such sensitivity to the empire because he is more interested that a Jewish Christian audience understand the details of Christ's fulfillment of the Old Testament prophecies.

People throughout the history of the Church have accepted both Gospels without particular difficulty. Luke narrates events of the circumcision of Jesus and the Presentation in the Temple, which would have occurred at precisely designated times soon after the birth of Jesus; Matthew's events of the Magi and the Flight into Egypt would have occurred afterward. Since the evangelists do not connect the different stories with each other, the Church has. Both writers focus on certain events and ignore others; our task is to better understand the mystery of faith that God has made in entrusting his Son, Jesus Christ, to the care of two loving human beings, and the journey of faith led by Mary and Joseph in their acceptance of God's word to them. Deeper understanding of these mysteries will help us live the mystery of our own life of faith, with its challenges, difficulties, and sorrows, looking forward to the ultimate goal of eternal life with God in heaven, along with the Blessed Virgin Mary and St. Joseph.

HEROD'S SUCCESSORS

In 7 B.C., Herod killed his two sons by Mariamme — Alexander and Aristobulus — by strangulation. He designated other sons by other wives and concubines as heirs, but he frequently changed his mind. In 5 B.C., Herod II, the son of Mariamme II, fell from grace after Herod divorced Mariamme II. He passed over his third son, Archelaus — the son of his Samaritan concubine, Malthace — because Archelaus' brother Antipater had accused him of treason. Then Herod made his youngest son, Antipas, another son of Malthace, his heir. Finally, Herod wrote a will in which he divided his kingdom among his three remaining sons: Antipas would rule Galilee and Peraea as tetrarch; Archelaus would rule Judea, Samaria, and Idumea as king; Philip, the son of another wife, Cleopatra of Jerusalem, would rule the territory east and northeast of Galilee as tetrarch (Josephus, *Jewish Antiquities*, xvii, 188-189). After Herod's death, the three sons went to Rome, where Caesar Augustus ratified Herod's will and divided his kingdom, a fact that would come into play throughout the Gospels.

STUDY

We now return to the last episode in the childhood of Jesus — the Finding in the Temple.

Stop here and read **Luke 2:41-52** in your own Bible.

The setting of this scene is the family's annual pilgrimage to Jerusalem for the Passover. Israel's Law required the men to go to Jerusalem three times a year: for Passover, Shavuot (Pentecost), and Succoth (Tabernacles — an autumn feast).

While Joseph and Jesus would be expected to attend since the Law laid this responsibility on the men, Mary was also present according to their custom. The next time Passover is mentioned in Luke it will be the occasion of the dramatic events of the Last Supper and Jesus' crucifixion.

Luke describes the specific events of this particular Passover, although the feast itself is not described, just as the specifics of the sacrifices at the Presentation in the Temple were not described. As in most liturgical ceremonies, the rituals were prescribed and followed as normal.

The distinctive component of that feast was that Jesus remained in Jerusalem while his parents traveled for a whole day with their "traveling party," probably fellow citizens from Nazareth and nearby towns. Failure to find Jesus causes them to leave their friends and return to Jerusalem to seek him — an event called the Third Sorrow of Mary.

They find Jesus in the Temple. However, the scene includes more than a lost twelve-year-old boy. He is among the teachers, who generally gathered at the colonnaded porticoes along the edge of the large, slightly trapezoidal area of the courtyards built by Herod the Great. Jesus listens to them, asks questions, and amazes the hearers because he comprehends their answers and apparently has some of his own. This scene marks the first time Jesus does any action in the Gospel. This part of the episode — the finding of Jesus — in later centuries becomes the Fifth Joyful Mystery of the Rosary. Mary's Third Sorrow and the Fifth Joy are inherently connected, as is frequently the case with the sorrows and joys of most people's lives.

In the days between Palm Sunday and Holy Thursday, Jesus will return to these same courtyards and teach again. However, at that point he will make the scribes, the Pharisees, and the Sadducees very upset, while the crowds will eagerly listen and enjoy when he bests his opponents. The episodes of that week will exemplify Simeon's words that Jesus will be "set for the fall and rising of many in Israel, and for a sign that is spoken against" (Lk 2:34).

Both Mary and Joseph see him and are astonished; the present scene of Jesus being so involved with learning and teaching amazes them. His activity appears to leave them out of consideration. Surprisingly, Mary is the one who speaks — and it is parallel to Simeon speaking to her rather than to Joseph. She begins by asking, "Son, why have you treated us so? Behold, your father and I have been looking for you anxiously" (Lk 2:48). Mary describes the anxious searching for Jesus by his father and mother. Her statement does not actually indict the boy Jesus for some specific wrongdoing but wonders why he acted as he did to them.

Mary's question is parallel to questions asked by a number of people in the Old Testament who are surprised at another person's behavior.

INVESTIGATE

"FEAR NOT" (NO. 3)

Look up the following passages and make notes on the people and reactions:

PASSAGE	NOTES
Genesis 12:18	
Genesis 20:9	

Genesis 29:25	
Exodus 14:11	
Numbers 23:11	
Judges 15:11	

The key to this whole passage is Jesus' double question: "How is it that you sought me? Did you not know that I must be in my Father's house?" (Lk 2:49). The first question expresses surprise at their anxiety in the first place. Their whole relationship to him has been characterized by a faith that called forth total trust in God, and therefore in him. They do not need to be anxious about him if they remain focused on the complete trust.

The second question implies that they ought to understand his mission as being more focused on God than on his family. Joseph and Mary had expected to find him among the relatives and acquaintances, but he thought they should expect him to be concerned with his Father's affairs. One amazing component of the answer is that he considers the Temple his Father's house. He will show similar proprietary claims when he cleanses the Temple of the sellers and money changers.

Finally, they "did not understand" what he said to them (Lk 2:50). Many parents — if not most — assume that their lack of understanding of something their child says is the fault of the child. It is not a far stretch to think that he or she may be foolish or even lying, and a common reaction is to punish the child when the parents do not understand. That is not his parents' reaction here. They simply returned to Nazareth, and Jesus was obedient to them. He had not been disobedient to them in the preceding action; he had taken an initiative to be about the far more important affairs of his heavenly Father, the Lord of the Temple.

As after the visit of the shepherds, "his mother kept all these things in her heart" (Lk 2:51). Such mysterious events were not easily understood by Mary because the mysteries originated in God's great plan of salvation. She did those things specifically asked of her and attended to the business of everyday life. Yet the events either happening around her Son or, in this case, done directly by him, would mystify her.

These reflections and memories of key events of Jesus' early life were so pondered and treasured by Mary that she related them to others, and the written text — a Semitic original that underlies the present Greek text — was passed on to the Church. These are not the random events that all parents remember — first steps, key events of transition from one stage of childhood to another, etc. — but are events that made more sense in the light of the rest of Jesus' life, death, and resurrection. Therefore, Mary's pondering in her heart gives us an important insight. Every Christian can learn to imitate this quality of the Virgin Mary so as to ponder the whole life of Jesus within the depths of his or her heart and thereby gain not only perspective on Jesus Christ but also on one's own life.

The concluding verse of the infancy and childhood narratives simply states that Jesus grew in wisdom, age, and grace.

DISCUSS

1. What new insights into the Magi and their significance to the story of salvation have you gained from this chapter?
2. When events of life trouble you, in what ways can Mary be an example of how to pray and "ponder in your heart"? How does her example help you think about your relationship to Jesus?
3. How does the finding in the Temple relate to the later event of Jesus' life when he drove out the money changers?

PRACTICE

This week, if there is some teaching of the faith that you find difficult to understand, ask Mary to help you ponder its truth and help you understand how its mystery originated in God's great plan of salvation.

Session 6

MARY IN CHRIST'S PUBLIC MINISTRY

> "If our faith is weak, we should turn to Mary. Because of the miracle at the marriage feast at Cana, which Christ performed at his mother's request, his disciples learned to believe in him (cf. John 2:11). Our mother is always interceding with her Son so that he may attend to our needs and show himself to us, so that we can cry out, 'You are the Son of God.'"
>
> — St. Josemaría Escrivá

The Blessed Virgin Mary neither appears very frequently nor is mentioned much during the public ministry of Jesus. The most significant event is the Wedding at Cana, appearing only in John's Gospel, which we will examine in the next chapter. Three kinds of mention occur in the three Synoptic Gospels — Matthew, Mark, and Luke. (They are called "synoptic" because they have the same basic view of Jesus' life and share many episodes and sayings, distinct from John's approach of few episodes and long discourses.) The first type deals with Jesus' mother and "brothers" seeking him out; the second is closely related to this but presents a woman's praise of Jesus' mother as the occasion of an important saying. The third situation simply mentions Mary while Jesus is at the synagogue in Nazareth.

 Stop here and read **Matthew 12:46-50** in your own Bible.

STUDY

Jesus' mother has not been mentioned in Matthew since 2:21, when Joseph brought her and the infant Jesus from Egypt to Israel. In addition, these verses (and the parallel passage in Mark 3:31-35) mark her sole appearance during Jesus' public life in Matthew's Gospel.

The scene opens with Jesus' mother and "brothers," none of whom are named, seeking to speak with him. No reason is given; just the request is described. They are standing outside, presumably outside the house where Jesus is staying in Capernaum and where his disciples are gathered to listen to him. An unnamed disciple informs him of his family's presence and tells him that they want to speak with him.

Jesus addresses this particular disciple with a question that is clearly meant to be heard by all the disciples: "Who is my mother, and who are my brethren?" (Mt 12:48). This seems odd, since their identity is clear; they are present to everyone. However, Jesus uses this rhetorical question to re-identify his family as anyone who "does the will of my Father in heaven" (Mt 12:50).

On the one hand, this episode is consistent with Jesus' behavior toward anyone he knows: his commitment to the will of the Father is more important than any consideration of personal relationship. When Peter, whom he has just called the rock upon which he would build his Church, rebukes Jesus for speaking about his coming suffering, death, and resurrection, Jesus rebukes him far more strongly: "Get behind me, Satan! You are a hindrance to me; for you are not on the side of God, but of men" (Mt 16:23; also Mk 8:33).

This is even consistent with the way Jesus treated Mary and Joseph when he was twelve: it was more important to be about his Father's business than to remain with their caravan. They did not understand the saying, but recall that Mary pondered it in her heart through the years when he remained subject to them.

On the other hand, the more important point is that Jesus identifies those who do the will of his Father as his mother, brothers, and sisters. He consistently demands that his disciples listen to his words in order to do them. He explains that a key to salvation is not a personal relationship with him but rather the choice of the human will to accept the graces God bestows and do his holy will. We are, as St. Paul teaches, "children of God." However, we are not children of God by our nature, as is taught by the FOGBOM adherents. This acronym stands for "the fatherhood of God and the brotherhood of man." While all humans share the same DNA — no matter what race or nation they might belong to, and therefore they are all brothers and sisters — that does not necessarily imply the fatherhood of God. Jesus Christ is the only-begotten Son of God (Jn 1:18; 3:16; 1 Jn 4:9), and only he is the Son of God by nature. We are children of God by adoption.

INVESTIGATE

CHILDREN OF GOD

 Look up the following passages and make notes on our relationship to the Father:

PASSAGE	NOTES
Matthew 7:7-11	
Matthew 7:21	

Matthew 21:28-31	
Romans 8:15-17	
Romans 8:19-23	
Galatians 4:4-7	

As a gift of the Holy Spirit, we are adopted children of God. As such, he offers us an inheritance of eternal life. However, as Jesus makes clear, we must also make our choice to do the will of the Father rather than our own will or the will of the culture around us. This is all the more significant in the larger context of the opposition Jesus faced in his public ministry. Clearly, the decision to do the Father's will stands over against the world's reaction to and rejection of Jesus. This is no less true in the modern world than it was in the first century.

STUDY

This same incident is also related in Mark's Gospel.

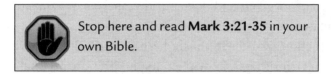

Stop here and read **Mark 3:21-35** in your own Bible.

The older RSV Bible reads "his friends" and a newer edition says "his family" went out to seize him, but the Greek phrase translates as "those around him." This phrase frequently refers to someone's envoys or adherents but sometimes can refer to a person's relatives. The context adds to the ambiguity, since the list of the Twelve immediately precedes these verses, but his mother and "brothers" are specifically mentioned in verse 31. The question is this: Were his disciples trying to protect him from the people who thought he was "beside himself," or was his family coming to seize him, perhaps to take him away from a compromised reputation? Since "those around him" were the people who "went out," and "his mother and his brothers ... [were] standing outside," while the disciples were the people on the inside, it seems logical to assume that the people who came to "seize" him were his relatives. The text does not state the place from which they "went out," which adds to the ambiguity of this text.

Next, Mark switches attention to a dialogue between Jesus and the Jerusalem scribes, who were the better educated among the Pharisee party (Mk 3:22-30). Some of them from Jerusalem opened up the discussion by accusing Jesus of being possessed by the "prince of demons."

Jesus poses the problem that if he were casting out demons by the power of Satan, then Satan's kingdom would be divided against itself and would be self-destructing. This is an argument against the charge that he casts out demons by the power of demons. Next, he explains his power to bind the "strong man" demons so that he can "plunder [the] house" — that is, take the possessed person outside the power of Satan's kingdom. This argument augments the first one.

Finally, since the scribes have accused Jesus of having an unclean spirit, they have blasphemed the Holy Spirit because they attributed a spiritual good — exorcism — to an evil spirit. Therefore, they are not able to be forgiven and have put themselves in a most dangerous place spiritually.

The section of our emphasis here is Mark 3:31-35, when Jesus' mother and "brothers" appear "outside" the crowd that is sitting around him. The text says nothing about trying to seize Jesus, which isn't in continuity with Matthew's version of the event. They simply ask for him and call him. The culmination of this passage is the saying that his mother and brothers and sisters are those who do the will of God, as in Matthew 12:50. Note the slight difference of wording: instead of "the will of my Father in heaven," here it is simply "the will of God."

CONSIDER

Next we move to a woman who cries out praise to Jesus' mother.

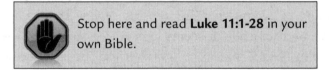

Stop here and read **Luke 11:1-28** in your own Bible.

This chapter of Luke opens with the disciples' request to teach them how to pray. Jesus begins with the Our Father and a teaching on confidence in prayer. After he casts out a spirit that is mute, most people marvel and others accuse him of having power over the evil spirits through Beelzebul, or else they want proof. This leads to his teaching on his power over the evil spirits, parallel to the teachings in Matthew 12:22-45 and Mark 3:22-30.

In this context, a woman says to Jesus, "Blessed is the womb that bore you, and the breasts that you sucked!" He replies, "Blessed rather are those who hear the word of God and keep it!" (Lk 11:27-28).

By proclaiming "blessed" the womb that bore him and the breasts that nursed him, this anonymous woman clearly exults in Jesus' power over demons and his ability to respond to the Pharisees who challenge him. As a woman who was probably a mother herself, she considers how blessed it would have been to bear and raise such a child. Of course, she proclaims blessedness for the Blessed Virgin Mary, most likely without knowing her by name. Her proclamation of beatitude is directed toward motherhood as made joyful by good children.

Jesus responds by redirecting the beatitude beyond maternal relationship, beyond the joy his mother had in raising him. Rather, blessed are all persons who hear God's word and keep it. This means that anyone can have the beatitude he proclaims, while the woman's blessing was directed to one person only.

Lumen Gentium (n. 58) talks about this, saying, "In the course of her Son's preaching she received the words whereby in extolling a kingdom beyond the calculations and bonds of flesh and blood, He declared blessed those who heard and kept the word of God (cf. Mk 3:35; Lk 11:27-28) as she was faithfully doing (cf. Lk 2:19, 51)."

Note that this refers to two passages that describe the Blessed Mother as having "kept" the words and events within her heart. The word translated in these two verses as "kept" (*suntereo, diatereo*) has nuances such as "preserve, treasure up," while a quite different word is used in Luke 11:28, meaning "keep, guard, watch over" (*phullasso*).

These texts show that Luke, of all evangelists, makes it clear that the Blessed Virgin Mary believed the words the Lord spoke to her through the angel Gabriel, and that she kept the events of the Nativity and the words of the child Jesus in the Temple, and indeed the rest of the events surrounding Jesus, treasured in her heart. In the context of these verses, Luke records Jesus' words about those who are blessed because they hear the word of God and keep it as an extension of his mother's activities to all Christians. Her relationship to Jesus is unique to her; her faith in God's word, her willingness to give her Fiat, and her life of treasuring the words in her heart are the model for all Christians. While his listeners could not know that, his words invited them into that faith relationship with God's word. We who read the whole of Luke's Gospel can pay attention both to Jesus' blessing for faith in God's word and keeping it, and we can look to Blessed Mary's example as a model for us all.

> "In these texts Jesus means above all to contrast the mother-hood resulting from the fact of birth with what this 'mother-hood' (and also 'brotherhood') is to be in the dimension of the Kingdom of God, in the salvific radius of God's fatherhood."
>
> — *Redemptoris Mater* (n. 21)

STUDY

Next we look at Jesus as he teaches in the Nazareth synagogue. This episode is related by both Mark and Matthew; Luke has another episode of a visit to the Nazareth synagogue, but that text focuses on the reading from Isaiah, his claim to have fulfilled it, and the subsequent rejection of the people of Nazareth. We will focus on the Matthew and Mark passages because both mention that he is the Son of Mary and, as in the preceding passages, mention his "brothers" and "sisters."

 Stop here and read **Matthew 13:53-58** and **Mark 6:1-6** in your own Bible.

In both texts, the main point is that Jesus' familiarity with the people of Nazareth made them take offense at his teaching in their synagogue. They used their knowledge of his relatives to dismiss him as a serious teacher. They looked to his occupation, which he learned from St. Joseph, as being a reason to question his ability to teach them, especially if he taught them with the same kind of authority that the people of the Capernaum synagogue had witnessed, or at the end of the Sermon on the Mount, or early in his mission at the Nazareth synagogue.

This is still a spiritual danger for those who have grown up within the Church. Some Christians have a type of familiarity with Jesus that makes them think they already know him, and that they can categorize him into a small, limited compartment of their lives. If this happens (as it does to many people), they will ignore Jesus because their familiarity does not draw them to have faith in him. No one should be surprised by this; children who live with their parents a certain number of years act in a similar way, particularly in adolescence or early adulthood. Usually, just as life experiences teach them that their parents were wiser than they once thought, so also life experiences teach people that they need faith in Jesus to become the full human beings in God's image and likeness that Jesus wants them to be. However, it is better to maintain loving, trusting faith in Jesus and not act like the doubting people of Nazareth.

CONSIDER

One of the big issues these passages bring up is the "brothers" and "sisters" of Jesus. It's important to ask the question: Are they Mary's children?

The Gospels offer similar information about Jesus through rhetorical questions:

In Matthew 13:55, he is the carpenter's son; in Mark 6:3, he is the carpenter. These statements are not contradictory but instead show that St. Joseph taught Jesus his trade and that both were carpenters.

Both Gospels name Mary as his mother.

Matthew 13:55-56 lists "his [brothers] James and Joseph and Simon and Judas" plus his unnamed "sisters," while Mark 6:3 mentions "James and Joses and Judas and Simon, and ... his sisters." The difference in ordering Simon and Judas is unimportant, and the difference between Joses and Joseph is due to transliterating a Semitic name into Greek.

It is also significant that each of these Gospels mentions some of the "brothers" and "sisters" only one other time — at the cross. However, it is not all of these relatives who are present but their *mother*, who is mentioned in a list of the women present as Jesus is dying.

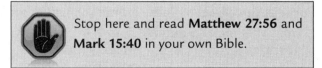

Stop here and read **Matthew 27:56** and **Mark 15:40** in your own Bible.

Note that the orthographic differences between Joseph and Joses remain consistent with both Gospels. Notice also that their mother is a woman named Mary, who is *not* identified as the Blessed Virgin Mary. This Mary is also mentioned by name in John as one of the women standing near the cross. Here she is identified as being the Blessed Virgin's "sister" and the wife of Clopas. The other Gospels mention neither the mother of Jesus nor John as being present during Jesus' crucifixion, but in John 19:35 the evangelist strongly asserts that he was personally present: "He who saw it has borne witness — his testimony is true, and he knows that he tells the truth — that you also may believe."

John also affirms the presence of Jesus' mother and her "sister" Mary, the wife of Clopas and the mother of Jesus' "brothers" James and Joses and his presumed "sister," Salome. These children of Clopas and his wife Mary, the "sister" of Jesus' mother, are called "brothers" and "sisters" in a society that uses these terms more loosely than moderns do. Terms for "cousin" do not exist, which is why Elizabeth is simply called a "kinswoman."

For example, in a translation of the Hebrew text of Genesis 13:8, Abram asks Lot rhetorically, "Are we not brothers?" We would say that they are uncle and nephew, since Lot is the son of Abram's brother, Haran. We simply accept the ancient (and contemporary) Semitic designation of brother and sister as including wider relationships. We cannot specify the precise relationship between the Virgin Mary and her "sister" Mary the wife of Clopas, and therefore we cannot be more precise about Jesus' relation to his "brothers" and "sisters." All that the Bible makes clear is that these "brothers" and "sisters" are the children of a certain Mary and Clopas and not of the Virgin Mary and Joseph.

DISCUSS

1. Jesus said that all who do the will of the Father are his family. Does this make a difference in how you view others in the world? Whom do you consider "family"?

2. How would you explain the question of Jesus' "brothers" and "sisters" to someone? Why is it important that Mary had no children other than Jesus?

3. When you read about how Jesus' family thought he was going a bit too far and tried to "rescue" him, how does that make you feel about your own faith? If you had lived at the time of Jesus, do you think you would have been one of his followers?

PRACTICE

This week, take some time to reread the verses about Jesus' family coming to get him. Place yourself in the scene. Are you one of his followers? Are you one of his family members? What are you thinking? What are you feeling? Consider the implications of FOGBOM — family of God, brotherhood of man.

Session 7

THE "WOMAN" IN JOHN'S GOSPEL

"In the public life of Jesus, Mary makes significant appearances. This is so even at the very beginning, when at the marriage feast of Cana, moved with pity, she brought about by her intercession the beginning of miracles of Jesus the Messiah (cf. Jn 2:1-11)."

— *Lumen Gentium* (n. 58)

The marriage feast at Cana marks the formal introduction of Jesus' public ministry. His mother plays an important role here, as it is her request that initiates the miracle of the transformation of water to wine.

> Stop here and read **John 2:1-12** in your own Bible.

John carefully enumerates the passing of the days from the time John the Baptist is questioned by priests and Pharisees until the wedding feast. "The next day" (Jn 1:29) after that incident, Jesus passes by and the Baptist identifies him as the Lamb of God. On the next day, Jesus passes by again and John the Baptist sends two disciples, one of whom is Andrew, to follow Jesus, and then he calls his brother Simon Peter. On the next day, they go to Galilee and find Philip, who then brings Nathanael of Cana to Jesus. Finally, after these four days, it is the "third day" (Jn 2:1), making the wedding occur at the end of the first week of Jesus' public ministry.

The primary purpose of the mention of the "third day" is to link this event with the immediately preceding beginning of the public ministry. However, identifying it as the "third day" also connects it with the Resurrection, which occurred on the "third day." Thus, the first miracle takes place on a third day, just as the greatest miracle did.

CONSIDER

It is common in traditional societies, especially religious ones, to make weddings large celebrations for family and friends because each wedding contains the promise of new life that will continue the family and the nation with new children. The enjoyment of meals and companionship, singing and dancing, and generous offers of gifts are aspects of so many Jewish and Christian weddings.

More secular ideas of weddings focus on the feelings of the couple, a romantic setting that suits them, vows that describe their feelings for each other, or an extravagance that augments the family's prestige through conspicuous consumption. The couple's mission from God, particularly their openness to having children, is frequently ignored in modern secular settings.

At this point, it is worth noting the presence of Jesus' mother at this wedding. Third-century Christians taught that Mary was a relative of the groom's mother, which cannot be proved but explains her presence at the wedding. In this context, it is useful to note that even though Mary conceived Jesus by the overshadowing of the Holy Spirit and without a man, after the conception she married Joseph. This made marriage the context for raising Jesus and shows the importance of marriage for her and for God's plan of salvation through Jesus.

Similarly, Jesus' presence, with his small group of four disciples (John, Philip, Peter, and Nathanael), blesses the wedding feast. They share in the celebration of this beginning of new family and its promise of new life. This has been a component of Christian appreciation of marriage as a sacrament that communicates God's grace and as the basic building block of society.

The Scriptures frequently describe the fulfillment of salvation and heaven itself as a wedding feast.

INVESTIGATE

HEAVEN AND WEDDINGS

 Look up the following passages and make notes on the marriage imagery:

PASSAGE	NOTES
Psalm 45	
Isaiah 62:4-5	
Hosea 2:19-20	

2 Corinthians 11:2	
Ephesians 5:31-32	
Revelation 19:7-9	
Revelation 21:2-4	

STUDY

The wine ran out at the wedding feast, which elicits a dialogue between Mary and Jesus. This conversation is rich with mystery, and each phrase evokes amazement the more deeply the phrases are considered.

"MOTHER OF JESUS"

This title reminds me of the way my Arab friends speak of one another as the "father of ..." or "mother of ..." a particular child, especially their firstborn sons. Everyone has a legal name by which most people identify the person. However, those friends who know the person more intimately might affectionately call them *Abu* ("father of") or *Um* ("mother of") a child. Even when the child is not yet born, the name comes from his grandfather, so already a married man (not an unmarried one) will be called "father of ..." The use of "Mother of Jesus" indicates such familiarity and respect for Blessed Mary.

Identified again as "the Mother of Jesus," she simply states that "they have no wine" (Jn 2:3). Note her sensitivity to the situation and its impact on others. It would be a great source of embarrassment for the hosts to be unable to provide wine at a wedding feast, and the mother of Jesus is concerned about them. Notice, too, that she does not tell Jesus to get wine for her or take her home before the feast gets boring. Rather, she focuses attention on the hosts' need to provide refreshment for the guests. At the same time, this statement of need implies a request, and Jesus will respond to her in those terms.

Her approach to Jesus introduces the notion of her role as Mediatrix (the feminine form of "mediator"). *Mediator* and *mediatrix* are Latin words derived from the word "medium," which means "middle." For that reason, a mediator or mediatrix is a person who stands "in the middle." Three references in Scripture ascribe the role of Mediator to Jesus Christ.

INVESTIGATE

 Look up the following passages and make notes on Jesus as Mediator:

PASSAGE	NOTES
1 Timothy 2:5-6	
Hebrews 9:15	
Hebrews 12:24	

However, Vatican II speaks of the Blessed Virgin Mary as a "co-mediatrix" in *Lumen Gentium* (n. 62):

> By her maternal charity, she cares for the brethren of her Son, who still journey on earth surrounded by dangers and difficulties, until they are led into the happiness of their true home. Therefore the Blessed Virgin is invoked by the Church under the titles of Advocate, Auxiliatrix, Adjutrix, and Mediatrix.

Having noted this, it is extremely important to remember that Mary's titles are to be understood in the context of her son, Jesus Christ, the one Mediator between God and humanity. This neither takes away anything from nor adds anything to the dignity and efficacy of Christ the one Mediator.

Lumen Gentium (n. 62) goes on to explain the way we can understand Mary's role in relationship to Jesus Christ, just as all other Christians also have some share in Christ's role as the Savior and in God's goodness that is shared by his creatures:

> For no creature could ever be counted as equal with the Incarnate Word and Redeemer. Just as the priesthood of Christ is shared in various ways both by the ministers and by the faithful, and as the one goodness of God is really communicated in different ways to His creatures, so also the unique mediation of the Redeemer does not exclude but rather gives rise to a manifold cooperation which is but a sharing in this one source.

Finally, the goal of Mary's subordinate role as Mediatrix is to help Christians come closer to Jesus Christ: "The Church does not hesitate to profess this subordinate role of Mary. It knows it through unfailing experience of it and commends it to the hearts of the faithful, so that encouraged by this maternal help they may the more intimately adhere to the Mediator and Redeemer" (*Lumen Gentium*, n. 62).

In John's Gospel, Mary approaches Jesus as the one between the human need for wine and her son's ability to act upon the need.

WINE OR GRAPE JUICE?

The Greek word used here is *oinos*, which is etymologically connected with the Latin *vinum*, from which comes the English word "wine." Some Christians have opted to abstain from all alcohol, as many monks and religious have done over the centuries (though not all, by any means), and some denominations consider wine and alcohol sinful. Therefore, they want to see that the concern here was for grape juice. However, in Genesis 9:20-21, Noah became "drunk" on wine (*oinos*), and in Ephesians 5:18, St. Paul warns people not to get "drunk" on wine (*oinos*). How can Scripture warn us against being drunk on grape juice? Clearly, *oinos* means wine, and that is what Jesus will miraculously make out of water.

CONSIDER

Jesus addresses his mother as "woman." He addresses a number of others using this word, including the Syro-Phoenician woman whose daughter was demon-possessed, a woman who had been bent over for eighteen years, the Samaritan woman at the well, the woman who had been caught in adultery, and Mary Magdalene.

It was a typical, polite form of address. However, there are no other examples of a son addressing his mother with this term, neither in biblical texts nor in Greek literature.

Jesus' unique use of "woman" as a form of address to his mother may be a reference to Adam's wife. Before the fall into original sin, she is simply called "the woman," as if this were her name; only after the Fall and the Lord's curses is she named Eve. By calling his mother "woman," Jesus can be said to address her by the name of the mother of the human race before she fell and was called "Eve." As such, this title may be seen as the recognition by Jesus, the New Adam, that his mother is the New Eve, but in terms of her being in the sinless state before the fall into original sin. Jesus will address his mother the same way when he is hanging on the cross, and this meaning may become even more significant there.

Jesus then goes on to say to her, "What have you to do with me?" (Jn 2:4) or "What to me and to you?" — the latter being a literal translation of an idiom that appears in both Hebrew and Aramaic. Interestingly, John uses Aramaisms such as this in dialogues, rather than in his narrative sections, indicating an interest in preserving dialogue that reflects the way people spoke rather than rephrase in good Greek grammar and idiom.

The Old Testament uses this idiom in two ways. One is negative, where it refers to situations of one party harming another and then asking what made the offended party deserving of bad treatment (see Judg 11:12; 1 Kings 17:18; 2 Chron 35:21). Demons use the expression in this way when they speak to Jesus in Mark 1:24, 5:7. The second usage is when one person is asked to get involved in a situation that is not his business (2 Kings 3:13; Hos 14:8). This is the meaning in John. Jesus does not want the lack of wine to be his concern at this point.

He then adds, in the same verse, "My hour has not yet come." This phrase needs to be seen in the context of other uses of Jesus' hour and time within the Gospel of John.

INVESTIGATE

HOUR AND TIME

Look up the following passages and make notes on Jesus' "hour" and "time":

PASSAGE	NOTES
John 7:6	
John 7:30-31	
John 8:20	

John 12:23-28	
John 13:1	

TIME VS. HOUR

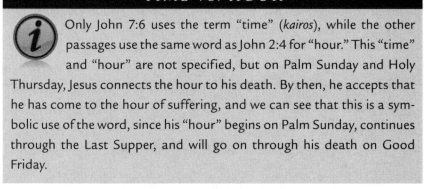

Only John 7:6 uses the term "time" (*kairos*), while the other passages use the same word as John 2:4 for "hour." This "time" and "hour" are not specified, but on Palm Sunday and Holy Thursday, Jesus connects the hour to his death. By then, he accepts that he has come to the hour of suffering, and we can see that this is a symbolic use of the word, since his "hour" begins on Palm Sunday, continues through the Last Supper, and will go on through his death on Good Friday.

At Cana, Jesus informs his mother that his hour has not yet come, and the performing of a miracle is implied in the beginning of the hour. She does not respond to that statement but leaves it hanging. However, it may be worth pointing out that this first miracle in which Jesus will change water into wine, occurs just before Passover, just as the multiplication of loaves and fish takes place just before Passover. These prefigure the institution of the Eucharist, where Jesus speaks with the same divine authority to transform bread into his sacred Body and wine into his precious Blood, which occurs at the third and final Passover in John's Gospel. It is also in John 13:1 that John informs the reader that "Jesus knew that his hour had come to depart out of this world to the Father." Therefore, both the term "hour" and the miracle of water into wine connect Cana with the Last Supper, the Eucharist, and the death on the cross. And again, at the cross Jesus' mother will appear for the last time in John's Gospel as she witnesses his "hour."

STUDY

Jesus' mother does not respond directly to Jesus' objection, but turns attention from him to the nearby servants, instructing them, "Do whatever he tells you" (Jn 2:5). She does not persist with cajoling or begging Jesus for a miracle at all. By telling the servants to obey Jesus, she makes an act of trust that he will do precisely whatever is the Father's will in regard to the need she presented and the proper arrival of his hour. The fact that she does not give him precise instructions on the manner in which to respond to her request implies that she accepts his wisdom in doing what is right. Furthermore, by instructing the servants to "Do whatever he tells you," she widens the scope of obedient trust in Jesus to these unnamed strangers.

> "The Mother of Christ presents herself as the spokeswoman of her Son's will, pointing out those things which must be done so that the salvific power of the Messiah may be manifested. At Cana, thanks to the intercession of Mary and the obedience of the servants, Jesus begins 'his hour.' "
>
> — *Redemptoris Mater* (n. 21)

Rather amazingly, the servants obey Jesus' words to fill the six jars, which entails a significant amount of labor — each stone jar contains 20 to 30 gallons, so the servants have to draw between 120 and 180 gallons of water in order to fill those jars. They also obey his instructions to draw out the water and give it to the chief steward of the feast, who would have been their actual boss. This may not have seemed very sensible to them, but they obey, just as Jesus' mother had told them to do.

The servants take the wine to the steward, which then provokes his words to the bridegroom who was the host of the feast. The steward does not understand the import of tasting the wine and identifying it as the best. The miracle is unknown to him, though the servants who have obeyed Jesus are well aware that a sign has taken place. The steward assumes that better wine has been kept until the end, and he reproves the groom for being somewhat foolish for withholding the good wine. John does not give the groom's response; his interest is in letting the readers know that Jesus' first sign was demonstrable to a person simply performing his duties as a steward, yet is unaware of any miracle. He acts as an objective observer. Yet he also testifies to the excellence of quality of the miracle, just as John and the other evangelists all point out the abundance of leftover bread and fish after the miracle of the multiplication.

CONSIDER

John, who would have been one of the disciples present at the wedding in Cana, informs the reader that this was the first of Jesus' "signs." He prefers the word "sign" over "miracle" or "wonder" because it emphasizes that each action points beyond itself to something more. This is especially clear in John 6, where the multiplication of loaves and fish points to the deeper reality of the Eucharist, as Jesus' instruction in that chapter indicates. No such explanation is given after the wedding at Cana, but the mention of the coming Passover in John 2:13 will point the Christian reader to the institution of the Eucharist at the Last Supper, which occurs at the third Passover in Jesus' public ministry. The "hour" is the time of Jesus' "glory," and by doing the sign that his mother requested, he began the hour that will lead to glory. Of course, this will be fulfilled on the cross and in the Resurrection, but this mystery begins at this point.

John sees this as the moment in which the disciples began to believe in Jesus. Their faith would need to grow considerably, and they would experience fear in Gethsemane, and Peter would deny him at Caiaphas' court, but they would all grow in faith in him, except Judas, whose being "a devil" and betrayal is first mentioned after Jesus taught about the Eucharist.

A concluding notice says that Jesus, his mother, and disciples moved to Capernaum for a few days. John's notification indicates Mary's awareness of Jesus' ministry in Capernaum and her knowledge of some of the people there. Not much more can be said.

STUDY

Finally, we will look at Mary at the Crucifixion. The primary focus will be on Jesus' words to his mother and his beloved disciple. However, it will be useful to give the setting for this event and add a couple of comments that are relevant to the Blessed Virgin Mary's place at Jesus' crucifixion.

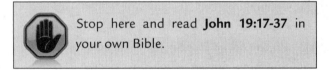

Stop here and read **John 19:17-37** in your own Bible.

The section begins by emphasizing a dispute about the title that was placed above Jesus' head on the cross to indicate his crime. Pilate insists on his phrase over the objections of the chief priests, who want to emphasize that he had merely claimed to be the King of the Jews, while they emphasized, "We have no king but Caesar" (Jn 19:15). This dispute was merely a power play between Pilate and the chief priests. However, if a reader of the whole New Testament recalls the annunciation by Gabriel, this title has another meaning for the Virgin Mary. Gabriel told her: "He will be great, and will be called the Son of the Most High; and the Lord God will give to him the throne of his father David, and he will reign over the house of Jacob for ever; and of his kingdom there will be no end" (Lk 1:32-33).

Yet, the first time she sees Jesus addressed as a king is in the title over his head as he hangs on the cross. This would hardly have been her image of kingship and rule over Israel as foretold by Gabriel. We can only imagine what a test of her faith in the angel's words this must have been.

When the soldiers then cast lots for Jesus' garments, John emphasizes that it is in fulfillment of Psalm 22, but one can only imagine what Jesus' mother would have thought. She had probably made those clothes for him with great tenderness and love. Seeing the garment as the object of casting lots and gambling would have struck her heart with great pain.

Next, we are told that "standing by the cross of Jesus were his mother, and his mother's sister, Mary the wife of Clopas, and Mary Magdalene" (Jn 19:25). This verse establishes the identities of the three women named Mary who stood by the cross of Jesus, though the evangelist does not give the proper name of Jesus' mother.

> "After this manner the Blessed Virgin advanced in her pilgrimage of faith, and faithfully persevered in her union with her Son unto the cross, where she stood, in keeping with the divine plan, grieving exceedingly with her only begotten Son, uniting herself with a maternal heart with His sacrifice, and lovingly consenting to the immolation of this Victim which she herself had brought forth."
>
> — *Lumen Gentium* (n. 58)

Standing at the cross is one of the most poignant moments in Blessed Mary's pilgrimage through life. Being chosen as the mother of the Redeemer did not lead to a triumphant journey of glory at every stage. Leaving the comfort of home in Nazareth to give birth in Bethlehem, traveling to Egypt to escape death, losing the child Jesus in the Temple, the redefinition of motherhood as belonging to those who obey God, and finally this horrible experience of witnessing her son die through crucifixion was essential to her vocation because it was essential to Christ's mission of redemption. The more we contemplate the cross from her perspective, the deeper will be our appreciation of all that it means. We can stand with her and the other women to learn more of the love for Jesus Christ at its greatest and deepest point.

It is at this point that Jesus once again calls his mother "woman," as he gives her care over to John. This title, which as mentioned above is unprecedented for a son addressing his mother in either Hebrew or Greek literature, appears more importantly connected to the first woman, Eve. This connection is highlighted by John in 19:41, noting: "Now in the place where he was crucified there was a garden, and in the garden a new tomb where no one had ever been laid." This sets Jesus, the "New Adam," and his mother, the "woman," in a garden and at a tree on a hill in that garden. Jesus hangs from the tree of the cross, not as the fruit of the tree of the knowledge of good and evil, but as Life personified, as frequently reported in John's Gospel.

INVESTIGATE

LIFE

 Look up the following passages and make notes on "Life":

PASSAGE	NOTES
John 1:4	
John 5:21	

John 5:26	
John 6:51	
John 11:25-26	
John 14:6	
John 17:3	

Through the centuries, theologians and preachers have portrayed the cross as the new "tree of life," and Jesus who hangs upon it is the life-giving fruit. His mother standing there at this new tree of life replaces the old Eve who grasped the tree of the knowledge of good and evil in direct disobedience and gave it to the first Adam. The New Eve, the woman, accepts what happens and what is said to her in faith, and becomes not "Eve," the mother of the living, but a mother to a beloved disciple.

As he is dying, Jesus entrusts Mary to the "disciple whom he loved," saying, "Woman, behold, your son" (Jn 19:26 — RSV-SCE).

Readers correctly assume that the "disciple whom he loved" was John, one of the first disciples who followed Jesus. He is called this only after Jesus' "hour" has come. Venerable Archbishop Fulton J. Sheen pointed out one significance of this designation by frequently saying that the use of John's name in this passage would have limited its importance to John only. However, by calling him the "disciple whom he loved," the Gospel opens up this event to every beloved disciple.

In that light, Jesus also opens his mother to a new motherhood, one that will embrace a beloved disciple and, eventually, all beloved disciples. Another way to see this is that Jesus entrusts the beloved disciple to his mother, and thereby entrusts every beloved disciple to her, all through history. Catholics have seen this as a passage in which Jesus bestows a tremendous gift upon every believer — his mother's care for them. Catholics and Orthodox Christians seek her intercession, not only because of the example of her petition to Jesus at Cana, but more importantly because he entrusts every beloved disciple to her. For that reason, they pray the Rosary, sing hymns to her, and dedicate themselves to her maternal love.

At the same time, Jesus says to the beloved disciple, "Behold, your mother!" (Jn 19:27). This will mean that his mother will move into John's home to live with him. However, again, this is an entrustment of his mother to every beloved disciple. All Christians can take her into their hearts and accept her motherly care. All Christians will speak well of her and in so doing fulfill her words, "Henceforth all generations will call me blessed." By adding this gift to the beloved disciple, Jesus makes the entrustment mutual between his mother and disciples.

JOHN AND MARY

Some apologists point out that if Mary had other children there would have been no need to entrust her to the care of the beloved disciple. Since Jesus' "brothers" are apparently the children of Clopas and a Mary known as the sister of Jesus' mother, one of his dying wishes was to entrust her to his beloved disciple.

At the end of his life, Jesus' side is pierced with a spear. Some Christian readers have connected the piercing of Jesus' side to the prophecy that Simeon spoke to the Virgin Mary in Luke 2:34-35: "Behold, this child is set for the fall and rising of many in Israel, and for a sign that is spoken against (and a sword will pierce through your own soul also), that thoughts out of many hearts may be revealed."

> "Truly, O blessed Mother, a sword has pierced your heart. For only by passing through your heart could the sword enter the flesh of your Son. Indeed, after your Jesus — who belongs to everyone, but is especially yours — gave up His life, the cruel spear tore open His side. Thus the violence of sorrow has cut through your heart, and we rightly call you more than martyr, since the effect of compassion in you has gone beyond the endurance of physical suffering."
>
> — St. Bernard of Clairvaux

On a natural level, one of the greatest pains and sorrows in life is the grief of a parent for a child who has died. Children, too, feel great grief when parents die, but the normal expectation of life is that children will someday bury their parents, honoring them to the end. Seeing a child die is contrary to the natural expectations of life, and the loss creates a hole in the heart where the beloved child once had a place. Parents who have lost children never cease feeling that emptiness. Standing by her son while he dies and witnessing the soldier piercing his side could not help but bring Simeon's prophecy to Mary's mind. Awareness of such a connection lies behind the bust of the Blessed Virgin Mary at the altar of the Thirteenth Station on Mount Calvary, which depicts seven swords piercing her heart, in honor of her Seven Sorrows. Similarly, one of the most beloved and therefore duplicated pieces of art is Michelangelo's Pieta inside St. Peter's in Rome. Such images draw us to experience the suffering and death of Jesus through his mother's eyes and with her heart. In this way, we can deepen our understanding of what it cost Jesus to grant us redemption from our sins.

MARY AT THE CROSS AND IN THE MASS

The key to understanding John and Mary at the cross is to understand that the moment of entrustment is able to be continued throughout history as we recall our Lady in the Eucharistic Prayer, precisely that part of the Mass that centers on the sacrifice on Calvary.

I have been given many opportunities to concelebrate the liturgy in seven of the Eastern Rites of the Catholic Church — Greek Catholic and Melkite, in the Byzantine tradition; Coptic, Chaldean, and the following branches of the Syriac-speaking Churches: Syriac Catholic, Syro-Malankara, and Maronite. I have bi-ritual faculties in the Maronite Catholic Church. I have also been privileged to attend Eastern Orthodox liturgies as a visitor. All of these branches of the ancient Church in Asia, Africa, and Europe use *anaphoras* (the Eastern term for Eucharistic prayers) that include explicit mention of the Blessed Virgin Mary and the saints. This practice is universal in the Churches that maintain the apostolic succession of bishops and priests, who believe in the Real Presence of Jesus Christ in the Eucharist, and who understand the Eucharist as the re-presentation of Christ's sacrifice on Calvary. Interestingly, the various Christian denominations that reject these precise elements of the theology of the Eucharist also omit mention of the Blessed Virgin Mary and the saints in their communion services or Lord's Supper services.

DISCUSS

1. What new insights into Jesus' calling his mother "woman" have you gained in this chapter? Has this changed your ideas about what was happening at Cana?

2. How is the "hour" that Jesus spoke about more relevant to you now, in the light of both his ministry and his death?

3. How do you understand Mary's role as Mediatrix? Why does her role not take anything away from Jesus' role as our Mediator?

Session 8

MARY AFTER JESUS' PUBLIC MINISTRY

> "But the power of Mary over all the devils will especially shine forth in the latter times, when Satan will lay his snares against her heel: that is to say, her humble slaves and her poor children, whom she will raise up to make war against him. They shall be little and poor in the world's esteem, and abased before all like the heel, trodden underfoot and persecuted as the heel is by the other members of the body. But in return for this, they shall be rich in the grace of God, which Mary shall distribute to them abundantly. They shall be great and exalted before God in sanctity, superior to all other creatures by their lively zeal, and so well sustained with God's assistance that, with the humility of their heel, in union with Mary, they shall crush the head of the devil and cause Jesus Christ to triumph."
>
> — St. Louis de Montfort

The last time we have an account of Mary's life is from Acts of the Apostles, although Mary has a number of roles in the early Church, ranging from her presence within the early Jerusalem community to a mention of her by St. Paul, as well as a role at the end of time in Revelation. Acts is the second volume of Luke's work. The first part of chapter one of Acts concerns a primary event in our salvation — namely, Jesus' ascension into heaven. This is followed by events concerning the life of the community of disciples in the Upper Room of the Last Supper and the Lord's appearances after the Resurrection.

There is also a listing of community members, along with an account of the death of Judas Iscariot and the selection of Matthias to replace him. After the listing of the eleven apostles comes a specific mention of "Mary the Mother of Jesus" (Acts 1:14).

 Stop here and read **Acts 1:1-26** in your own Bible.

Mary and the "brothers" of Jesus who had wanted to speak with him during the public ministry are now present in the Upper Room, in prayer together with the other disciples who came to do the will of the Father (Mt 12:50; Mk 3:35). Most interesting is the fact that Luke, who particularly emphasized that "the Holy Spirit will come upon you, and the power of the Most High will overshadow you" (Lk 1:35) at the incarnation of Jesus, now mentions Mary's presence in prayer for the coming of the Holy Spirit promised by Jesus. *Lumen Gentium* (n. 59) highlights this connection as well, saying that we also see "Mary by her prayers imploring the gift of the Spirit, who had already overshadowed her in the Annunciation."

THE FIRST NOVENA

 Luke tells us that the apostles, the women, and Jesus' "brothers" and mother devoted themselves to prayer in the time between the Ascension and Pentecost. Often this experience of the Church at prayer for these nine days is cited as the first novena. Up to the present day, the practice of nine days of prayer has been used for various specific needs, and often it is prayed with a petition for the intercession of the Blessed Virgin Mary and/or some other saint, also in imitation of the community of apostles and disciples in the Upper Room, many of whom are still celebrated by name as saints and patrons.

STUDY

Obviously, Mary's experience of being overshadowed by the Holy Spirit so that God the Son could be virginally conceived in her womb was a one-of-a-kind experience, and in the Upper Room she prays for a gift of the Holy Spirit that will be general for the whole Church on Pentecost. Yet her experience does offer a model for the Church as a whole and for the individual Christian. The whole Church will become "one body" (the body of Christ), by the power of the Holy Spirit (1 Cor 12:4-13). Each individual will have specific gifts from the Holy Spirit, but the Holy Spirit will also unite all the members to form a body, a single community that is characterized as being like Jesus Christ.

However, the goal of the individual Christian life is that "Christ be formed" in each person (Gal 4:19). While Jesus Christ does not take on a new human nature within each Christian as he did in the womb of the Virgin Mary, the Holy Spirit does seek to form the image of Jesus Christ within each person so that all can become "a new creation" in Christ (2 Cor 5:17) and live out the rest of their lives like him. In other words, the Holy Spirit effects a true transformation of each Christian. This transformation will grow and develop over time as each individual accepts the grace of the Holy Spirit and cooperates with the transformation he effects. Still, the goal of the Holy Spirit is for each person to become like Jesus Christ. For that reason, the incarnation of Jesus Christ within Mary's womb is a type, or model, of what the Holy Spirit accomplishes within each Christian, and therefore Mary's prayer is especially noteworthy, as Acts 1:14 brings out.

The Blessed Virgin Mary is not mentioned by name elsewhere in Acts. The main point of the text is to present the ministries of St. Peter and especially St. Paul, perhaps to defend them in Rome from various accusations. However, a small note about the life of the Church would have included Blessed Mary and may be helpful for our reflection: "And they devoted themselves to the apostles' teaching and fellowship, to the breaking of bread and the prayers" (Acts 2:42).

Two points of interest regarding Mary are the devotion to the apostles' teaching and the breaking of the bread. Though explicit evidence is not present in the scriptural texts, we can surmise that at some point the Blessed Virgin shared her deep reflections on Jesus' infancy and childhood with members of the community. It is impossible to know the precise identity of the person or persons with whom she shared the information or when she did so. All that scholars can determine is that the material was originally passed on in Aramaic before inclusion in Luke's Gospel. In some way, the Virgin Mary influenced the teaching of the apostles about Jesus' birth, and ever since their time this has influenced the faith of Christians.

The second surmisal is that the Blessed Virgin attended the "breaking of the bread" (a term that Luke uses for the Eucharist) with the early Church. She would have heard Peter, John, and the other apostles pronounce Jesus' Eucharistic words, "This is my body." One cannot help but wonder at the kind of faith these words evoked in the heart of the woman in whose womb the body of the unborn Jesus took shape. Perhaps a reflection on the intentness with which the Blessed Mother would have gazed at the Eucharistic Body and Blood of her beloved son, Jesus, and then received him in the Eucharist might help all Christians to a new awareness of their own attentiveness to the presence of Jesus in the Eucharist.

CONSIDER

The last direct mention of Mary as Jesus' mother is by Paul in his epistle to the Galatians. In it, he never mentions her by name, only saying that the Son is "born of woman" (Gal 4:4). However, this passage is filled with important points, not only for that phrase but also for the variety of lessons contained in the whole text.

 Stop here and read **Galatians 4:1-7** in your own Bible.

This section is part of a longer discussion in Galatians in which St. Paul teaches that faith in Jesus Christ, rather than works of the Law (that is, the first five books of the Bible, known as the Torah or Pentateuch), saves a person because it unites one to Jesus. However, he explains that the Law has a purpose in Israel's history, since God would not have revealed it if it were meaningless or useless. He uses the image of a young child who has an inheritance due to him, but because he is a minor incapable of handling the responsibilities of owning property, his father places guardians over him.

Paul then says that humanity was enslaved to the "elemental spirits of the universe" (*stoichea tou kosmou*), which does not include the word "spirits" but refers perhaps to the basic elements of the universe (earth, water, air, and fire), or, more likely, to the elemental, basic teachings of the world, which, for Paul are the basic principles of life in the Mosaic Law. This fits his comparison of the Law to a pedagogue in charge of an heir until he comes of age.

However, the fullness of time he speaks of in Galatians 4:4 refers to the maturity of the human race, which entails a change in status from being like children who are treated as slaves under the Law to a mature state during which the Son of God is born of woman for their redemption and adoption.

This adoption makes us children of the Father, and by his Spirit we can call God "Abba, Father." Jews did not often refer to God as their Father, but this new kind of relationship becomes possible as a gift of the Holy Spirit, the same Spirit by whom Mary conceived Jesus in her womb, and the Spirit promised by the Son at the Last Supper and before the Ascension.

Notice also that in the context of mentioning the Father's mission of the Son, who is "born of woman," the next stage is the revelation of the Blessed Trinity. God sent the Spirit of his Son "into our hearts" (Gal 4:6) because the life of these three Persons is not simply an abstract theological proposition but a fact of the spiritual life of each Christian. The Holy Spirit does not enter human hearts on his own private initiative but as a mission from the Father in union with the Son. As a result, the Holy Spirit empowers the Christian to cry out to God, "Abba! Father!" (Gal 4:6) — not merely as words but as the definition of a new relationship by which the Christian calls God by the very name Jesus Christ used for God: Father. In fact, he taught his disciples to address God as Father in the prayer he taught them. One cannot underestimate the importance of the power of the Holy Spirit in enabling the Christian to call God "Father," exactly as he empowers the Christian to call Jesus "Lord." In other words, the personal relationship with the Father and with Jesus Christ as Lord is possible only because of the interior relationship with the Holy Spirit within the human heart.

At the same time, this new relationship with the Persons of the Blessed Trinity bestows a new dignity on human beings. They are changed from the status of slaves to that of God's children and heirs of eternal life. The interpersonal relationship with God elevates the dignity of human beings and offers a vision of eternal glory in Christ Jesus as an inheritance that belongs to the children of God.

STUDY

Finally, we cannot end our examination of Mary in Scripture without looking at the "woman clothed with the sun" in the Book of Revelation (12:1).

Revelation is a complex text, largely because it speaks of a future end of the world in symbols. So far in history, the various attempts to date the Second Coming of Christ based on interpreting the evidence of Revelation in terms of contemporary events have been wrong. People frequently think that the catastrophes of their own era signal the end of the world — the repeated sack of Rome in the fifth century, the corruption in the Church in the sixteenth century or the rise of the Protestant Reformation, the World Wars, and late-twentieth-century cultural crises. Based on these failures to predict accurately, plus our Lord's teaching that even the angels do not know the day or hour, I always say that the end of the world is a management issue, and God is management; I'm in sales, so I do not know.

However, that does not relegate Revelation to a no-read category. The book contains much that is important about Jesus, the nature of the Judgment, the hope of heaven, the role of the saints and angels in heaven as intercessors, and other important points. One such issue is John's vision of the "woman clothed with the sun."

 Stop here and read **Revelation 12:1-6** in your own Bible.

The opening scene of this chapter has three distinct parts that introduce the major characters. First is a description of the woman. The woman is a "portent," or "sign" (*semeion*), in heaven. Particularly relevant for this passage is that Isaiah told King Ahab, who had refused to ask for a sign, "Therefore the Lord himself will give you a sign. Behold, a young woman shall conceive and bear a son, and shall call his name Immanuel" (Is 7:14).

SIGN FROM HEAVEN

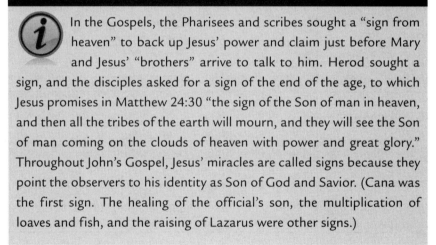

In the Gospels, the Pharisees and scribes sought a "sign from heaven" to back up Jesus' power and claim just before Mary and Jesus' "brothers" arrive to talk to him. Herod sought a sign, and the disciples asked for a sign of the end of the age, to which Jesus promises in Matthew 24:30 "the sign of the Son of man in heaven, and then all the tribes of the earth will mourn, and they will see the Son of man coming on the clouds of heaven with power and great glory." Throughout John's Gospel, Jesus' miracles are called signs because they point the observers to his identity as Son of God and Savior. (Cana was the first sign. The healing of the official's son, the multiplication of loaves and fish, and the raising of Lazarus were other signs.)

The sign of this woman is that she is "clothed with the sun." One way to understand the description is that it is a symbolic expression of the angel Gabriel's words: "The Lord is with you" (Lk 1:28). This is an image that makes sense in the light of other biblical passages, and is most relevant, because Revelation 21:23 reads: "[T]he city has no need of sun or moon to shine upon it, for the glory of God is its light, and its lamp is the Lamb." John equates the glory of God with the light of the sun, and the impression of being clothed with the sun may symbolize the surrounding presence of God.

Certain Old Testament passages say something similar about God.

INVESTIGATE

THE SURROUNDING PRESENCE OF GOD

 Look up the following passages and make notes on how God is described:

PASSAGE	NOTES
Psalm 84:11	
Isaiah 60:19-20	
Malachi 4:2	

Next, the moon is "under her feet" (Rev 12:1). No Old Testament texts explain this, but it clearly shows that she has a queenly rule in the heavens. Middle Eastern religions saw the moon as a male deity, while Greco-Roman religion saw it as a female deity. Here the moon is no deity but merely the place upon which the woman stands. The crown of twelve stars adds to her queenly image, with the number twelve being common to Israel's number of founding patriarchs and Christ's number of founding apostles. If these groups of men are the meaning of the twelve, then they have become the heavenly woman's crown.

She is with child and cries out in anguish in her labor. The image of birth pangs is used as a symbol of the travail and suffering at the end of time. Perhaps the mention of her birth pangs is meant to link this vision with the end-times concerns of the whole Book of Revelation.

> Stop here and read **Matthew 24:8, Mark 13:8**, and **1 Thessalonians 5:3** in your own Bible.

THE WOMAN AS SYMBOL

 Certain Fathers of the Church, such as Hippolytus, saw the woman as a sign of the Church; some moderns, especially Protestant commentators, see her as the people Israel. However, the Church did not give birth to Christ; he brought the Church into existence. Also, a nation does not get pregnant with a child; an individual woman does. Understanding the woman as a collective is therefore problematic, though she can easily be a symbol of both the Church and Israel.

> "By reason of the gift and role of divine maternity, by which she is united with her Son, the Redeemer, and with His singular graces and functions, the Blessed Virgin is also intimately united with the Church. As St. Ambrose taught, the Mother of God is a type of the Church in the order of faith, charity, and perfect union with Christ. For in the mystery of the Church, which is itself rightly called mother and virgin, the Blessed Virgin stands out in eminent and singular fashion as exemplar both of virgin and mother....
>
> "The Church indeed, contemplating her hidden sanctity, imitating her charity, and faithfully fulfilling the Father's will, by receiving the word of God in faith becomes herself a mother. By her preaching she brings forth to a new and immortal life the sons who are born to her in baptism, conceived of the Holy Spirit and born of God. She herself is a virgin, who keeps the faith given to her by her Spouse whole and entire. Imitating the mother of her Lord, and by the power of the Holy Spirit, she keeps with virginal purity an entire faith, a firm hope, and a sincere charity."
>
> — *Lumen Gentium* (nn. 63, 64)

STUDY

Next, the dragon, who stands in an aggressive posture to destroy the child to whom the woman is about to give birth, is introduced. He is described as "great" and "red," the color of blood and a symbol of death. The description of the seven heads and ten horns appears in Revelation 13:1, 3 and in 17:9-10, where these symbols are explained: "[T]he seven heads are seven mountains on which the woman is seated; they are also seven kings, five of whom have fallen, one is, the other has not yet come, and when he comes he must remain only a little while."

This description refers to the imperial capital city of Rome and its emperors, but it is a heavenly sign that will become an earthly reality later, associated with another woman, the wicked whore of Babylon.

The dragon has two actions. He acts on a cosmic level, sweeping down a third of the stars. Some of the Church Fathers saw this as an image of the angels who took the side of Satan in the rebellion and therefore concluded that a third of the angels fell with him.

The dragon's second action is to wait for the birth of the woman's child so as to devour him. The dragon is the child's enemy, and a dangerous enemy at that. In this context, we can connect this to Herod's attempt to destroy the infant Jesus soon after his birth and to Herod's failure because the angel of the Lord had instructed Joseph to take the child and his mother to Egypt until Herod's death. In addition, we can link the dragon's threat of the child's destruction to certain texts about Judas.

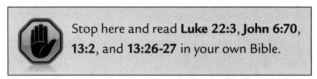

Stop here and read **Luke 22:3**, **John 6:70**, **13:2**, and **13:26-27** in your own Bible.

In this context, we might recall some points from the discussion of the angel Gabriel's description of the Virgin Mary's child as the "Son of the Most High" (Lk 1:32). The designation of God Most High appears in a number of Old Testament texts, but the highest density of repetition occurs in Daniel, where the Most High is the judge of his people. The Son of Man is introduced as the one to whom "was given dominion and glory and kingdom, that all peoples, nations, and languages should serve him; his dominion is an everlasting dominion, which shall not pass away, and his kingdom one that shall not be destroyed" (Dan 7:14).

Of course, "Son of Man" becomes the title most frequently used by Jesus to refer to himself in the Gospels, particularly in describing his role at the end of the world, as well as other situations where he has authority. The Son of Man and God Most High engage in the great battle against apocalyptic beasts and their final judgment in Daniel 7. Revelation 12 may be seen as part of the background to the final conflict between the woman's son, who rules the nations, and the red dragon and his angels.

At this point, Revelation describes the decisive action of the male child's birth, his escape to heaven, and the woman's success-ful flight to safety. The dragon makes no move as the woman brings forth a male child. This child will rule "all the nations with a rod of iron" (Rev 12:5), a clear reference to the messianic Psalm 2:8-9. Very briefly, the text summarizes the child's life as being "caught up to God and to his throne" (Rev 12:5). The child is obviously the Lord Jesus — and his life, ministry, death, and resurrection are passed over, with the emphasis on being taken up to heaven in the Ascension. Then the passage talks about the woman, whose place for being nourished for the predetermined time of 1,260 days was prepared for her on earth by God himself, in anticipation of the dragon turning his attention to attack her.

STUDY

The scene shifts dramatically from signs in heaven to a war in heaven. It is important to note that the dragon is here identified as "the ancient serpent" (Rev 12:9), a clear reference to the serpent in Genesis who had successfully tempted the first woman. He is further identified in the same verse as "the Devil and Satan, the deceiver of the whole world." This heavenly battle becomes the occasion for removing any mask so that all can understand the real nature of the serpent.

Stop here and read **Revelation 12:7-17** in your own Bible.

Though the dragon has his own army of angels, St. Michael and his angels thoroughly defeat them, forcing the evil spirits to leave their place in heaven. The assumption that Satan had a place in heaven is derived from both Old and New Testaments. Job 1-2 depicts Satan as having ready access to the Lord's heavenly court, since he has to ask the Lord's permission to tempt Job. However, the fall of Satan from heaven is mentioned by Jesus when the disciples return from their successful preaching mission: "I saw Satan fall like lightning from heaven" (Lk 10:18).

Later texts mention the fall of the host of evil angels.

INVESTIGATE

Look up the following passages and make notes on the fallen angels:

PASSAGE	NOTES
Ephesians 6:12	
1 Peter 5:8-9	
2 Peter 2:4	
Jude 1:6	

After this great battle comes a liturgical celebration of the victory in heaven. The announcement of the arrival of "salvation." "The power and the kingdom of our God and the authority of his Christ" (Rev 12:10) is linked directly to Satan's being cast down. His role as "accuser" is directly related to the Hebrew meaning of the word "Satan" and to the Greek term *diabolos*, or "devil," which means a "prosecuting attorney," in contrast to the Paraclete, which means a "counselor" or lawyer for the defense. While God the Father is the Judge, Satan accuses people, and Jesus the Paraclete and the Holy Spirit the Paraclete will defend the Christian from Satan's accusations. Therefore, the power behind the protection of Christians is the "blood of the Lamb," Jesus Christ, and the "word of their testimony," their own act of faith put into words (Rev 12:11).

Revelation then says that heaven and its citizens are to rejoice at Satan's defeat, but the people on earth experience "woe," a word of lamentation used for those who are dead or are doomed to die. The reason for their woe is Satan's defeat and his great wrath over his defeat. Earth is being warned that Satan's wrath will now be directed against it and its inhabitants. The dragon will attack the woman and the rest of her children. Through the centuries, people have read this passage in light of God's curse on the ancient serpent in Genesis 3:15, where he decrees: "I will put enmity between you and the woman, and between your seed and her seed." This enmity at the beginning continues until the end, and characterizes the history of the Church.

But Satan does not win. The woman is given two wings of an eagle so that she might fly from the serpent to a place where she is to be nourished. The bestowal of wings to the woman reminds us of the Lord's proclamation when Israel gets to Sinai: "You have seen what I did to the Egyptians, and how I bore you on eagles' wings and brought you to myself" (Ex 19:4). Bearing the nation on eagles' wings to escape enemies was God's work, and so it is for the woman in this passage.

Next, the dragon attempts a second time to kill the woman, this time by drowning her with a river of water that spews from his mouth — an attack that fails because the Lord is stronger than the

146

waters of chaos and is the force behind the earth when it swallows the dragon's destructive river to save the woman.

Finally, the dragon attacks the woman's other children — those who keep God's commandments and bear testimony to Jesus Christ. Here again we see reflections of Genesis 3:15: "I will put enmity between you and the woman, and between your seed and her seed." The focus is on the attack against her seed, since the dragon makes "war on the rest of her offspring" (Rev 12:17). The connection is in fact very direct, since the word translated here as "offspring" is actually "seed" (*spermatos*). This makes especially clear that the woman of this chapter is the New Eve, though the word "woman" is used because that was the first woman's name before the fall into sin; "Eve" was given to her as a name after the Fall.

Another important point here is that her children are characterized as "those who keep the commandments of God and bear testimony to Jesus" (Rev 12:17). They are not physically her seed, which would be very odd anyway since "seed" (*sperma* in Greek) refers to the male contribution to the conception of a child. Rather, they are her spiritual children because of their relationship to God and to Jesus, who is in fact this woman's son who wields the iron rod in Revelation 12:5. Because the children have a spiritual relationship to the woman, it has been quite natural to connect this passage with the one in which Jesus designates his mother as a mother to the beloved disciple, and the beloved disciple as a son to his mother.

CONSIDER

Christians have readily made this verse, Revelation 12:17, an important building block in Mariology. Parallel to the various texts in which God took the initiative to involve the Virgin Mary in taking a role in the history of salvation (the Annunciation, the Nativity, the words of Simeon in the Temple, the words of Jesus from the cross) are the ways in which the dragon initiates war against her and her spiritual children. However, over the centuries her spiritual children have learned from this passage that God took care of her and protected her from the evil dragon. Therefore, they seek out her prayers and want to imitate her example in their own experiences of being confronted by the evil one.

DISCUSS

1. How does the descent of the Holy Spirit upon Mary and the disciples at Pentecost relate to the overshadowing of the Holy Spirit at the Annunciation? What does this mean to you in your own life?
2. What are some new concepts or ideas about Mary as "the woman" in Revelation that you have learned from this study?
3. What role does Mary play in the "end times"? What are your thoughts about the "end of days"?

PRACTICE

This week, consider how God took care of the woman and protected her from the dragon. Think of some of the ways in which God has taken care of you and protected you from evil forces. Spend a few minutes in prayer, before the Blessed Sacrament if possible, thanking God for his protection in the past and asking for his guidance in the future.

Session 9

THE INTERCESSION
OF MARY

> "Placed by the grace of God, as God's Mother, next to her Son, and exalted above all angels and men, Mary intervened in the mysteries of Christ and is justly honored by a special cult in the Church."
>
> — *Lumen Gentium* (n. 66)

Among Christians who reject devotion to the Blessed Virgin Mary, objections based on theological ideas are common. Just as often, Catholics who defend devotion to Mary as our Lady are speaking about their relationship with the mother of Jesus Christ, whom they love as their spiritual mother. An important step to dialogue is the recognition of these two distinct approaches and a development of respect for each one.

However, the Catholic Church has developed a rich theology of devotion to Mary and the importance of her intercession, which needs to be understood in the context of the intercession of all the saints. Since many non-Catholics depend on the *"sola Scriptura"* approach to doctrine, we do well to show that devotion to the saints, including the Blessed Virgin Mary, is a scriptural teaching that does not deny the unique role of Jesus Christ as the Mediator between God and all people; indeed, it is a scripturally based teaching that all Christians would do well to heed. We will therefore examine Christ's role as Mediator, the role of intercession, and the particular intercessory role of the saints in heaven, including the Blessed Virgin Mary.

STUDY

The Catholic Church most definitely proclaims the scriptural truth of two Paracletes who intercede for us: Jesus Christ and the Holy Spirit.

 Stop here and read **John 2:1**, **3:16**, **15:26**, and **16:7** in your own Bible.

As Advocate or Paraclete, Jesus intercedes for us. Similarly, the Holy Spirit, the "other Paraclete," intercedes for us as well, as Romans 8:26 explains: "Likewise the Spirit helps us in our weakness; for we do not know how to pray as we ought, but the Spirit himself intercedes for us with sighs too deep for words." These simple and clear theological points are the basis for the structure of the official prayers of the Mass and other sacraments, as seen in the Roman Missal, the official Mass book. These prayers address the Father through the Son in the Holy Spirit at every Mass, including feasts of Mary and the saints. Never do these official prayers pray in the name of Mary or any other saint, "[f]or there is one God, and there is one mediator between God and men, the man Christ Jesus, who gave himself as a ransom for all" (1 Tim 2:5-6).

However, since we believe that death brings us to life with Christ, seeing him face-to-face and becoming like him, we can pray and intercede for others as he does. In fact, 1 Timothy 2:1-2 commands everyone to make petitions, prayers, intercessions, and thanksgivings on behalf of all men.

INVESTIGATE

PRAYING FOR OTHERS

 Look up the following passages and make notes on the need to pray and intercede for one another:

PASSAGE	NOTES
2 Corinthians 9:14	
2 Corinthians 13:7-9	
Ephesians 6:18-19	
Colossians 1:3-4, 9	
Colossians 4:2-3	

1 Thessalonians 5:16-18	
2 Thessalonians 3:1-2	
James 5:16	

CONSIDER

Obviously, the Bible shows how important it is to ask for prayers from fellow Christians, and equally clear is the fact that no passage in the Bible orders or forbids us to pray to the saints in heaven for their intercession. The Catholic Church does not force its members to have devotion to the saints but recommends it, on the basis of Scripture, and prohibits anyone from condemning it because Scripture urges believers to have devotion to the saints and seek their intercession.

 Stop here and read **Hebrews 12:22-24** in your own Bible.

This passage proclaims that we Christians have approached a variety of beings who dwell in heaven, which the author of Hebrews identifies as "the heavenly Jerusalem": the angels, God the Judge, the firstborn enrolled in heaven, the "spirits" of the righteous ones who have been made perfect, and Jesus, the Mediator.

According to the Catholic Church, a "saint" is the "spirit" of a person who has died and gone to heaven because he or she has been made righteous by God's grace and has been made perfect. Hebrews instructs us to approach these saints — just as we approach the angels, God the Judge of all, and Jesus the Mediator and his Blood of the New Covenant — because they are part of the new life we live.

In addition, two texts from Revelation describe the acts of intercession by the saints and angels in heaven.

 Stop here and read **Revelation 5:8** and **8:3-4** in your own Bible.

While Hebrews instructs Christians to approach the myriads of angels and the spirits of the righteous who have been made perfect, the passages in Revelation inform us about what the angels and saints do for us in heaven. The heavenly saints and angels accept "the prayers of the saints" like nuggets of incense in golden bowls. Incense smells quite good while it is still in nugget form, but once it is set on fire its aroma is released. This is the meaning of this image for the role of the saints, including the Blessed Virgin Mary, in bringing our prayers before the Lord at his heavenly throne. They are close to the Lord, and they take our incense-like prayers and set them on fire before the Lord, thereby releasing their sweet smell. Such is a biblical image of the mediation of the saints and angels.

Furthermore, just as Christians still living on earth are instructed many times to make intercession for one another, so also do the saints in heaven continue their ministry of intercession, though in heaven they can see the Lord God directly, instead of "in a mirror dimly" as during their earthly existence, as said in 1 Corinthians 13:12.

CONSIDER

The approach to the saints (the spirits of the perfected righteous ones) is mentioned in the midst of our approach to God the Judge and Jesus the Mediator. Likewise, Mary's intercession occurs in the context of Christ's mediation and in order to show its power, as it was manifested at Cana. Her role does not come from some inherent power in her nature but instead depends on God's disposition, just as the intercession of a fellow Christian on earth is effective because of God's dispositions rather than some inherent power of the Christian. Furthermore, Christ's mediation is the primary power between God and humans, but he gives people a share in his power. Therefore, as every Christian who intercedes for other people knows, praying for people helps draw one closer to Jesus Christ. The closeness to Jesus that the saints have in heaven is the basis for their power in intercession.

Lumen Gentium (n. 62) further explains Mary's maternal relationship with all Christians on the basis of her having taken a role in the history of salvation:

> This maternity of Mary in the order of grace began with the consent which she gave in faith at the Annunciation and which she sustained without wavering beneath the cross, and lasts until the eternal fulfillment of all the elect. Taken up to heaven she did not lay aside this salvific duty, but by her constant intercession continued to bring us the gifts of eternal salvation. By her maternal charity, she cares for the brethren of her Son, who still journey on earth surrounded by dangers and cultics, until they are led into the happiness of their true home.

It is Jesus Christ the Mediator who adds to the dignity of his mother, Mary, just as he adds to the dignity of every Christian who prays, whether on earth or in heaven. However, the dignity that Jesus Christ bestows on his mother is distinctive because of the tremendous faith she lived in the journeys from the Annunciation at Nazareth to Calvary in Jerusalem, and because of the love she showed

Jesus as his mother. God will always be more generous to us than we are to him, and that also applies to his mother Mary.

The reason for Catholic devotion to the saints is always twofold: we seek their intercession, and we want to imitate them. These two aspects are united in Catholic devotion to the Blessed Virgin Mary.

Meditating on and treasuring the mysteries of faith is exactly what Blessed Mary did herself. Therefore, the Church urges all believers to imitate her through deep contemplation and to trust that in so doing one's faith will grow. When Christian contemplation of Mary deepens, the result is the ability to hear her say about Jesus, her son: "Do whatever he tells you" (Jn 2:5).

By devotion to Mary, we come to recognize the unique divine power God has to cause the conception of his Son in a virgin's womb. That is meant to evoke wonder and amazement in all who hear about it and to direct their adoration to God for effecting such a miracle. At the same time, it is only logical to love the woman who believed in God's infinite power and accepted that *with God nothing is impossible.* She accepted God's will in love, and those who contemplate her come to love her and the will of God more. Such is the goal of deeper reflection and meditation on the Scriptures that treat of Mary's role in the salvation of the world, as well as of deeper devotion to her.

DISCUSS

1. How would you explain the Church's theology to someone who claims that Catholics pray "to" Mary and that Mary is the one who answers prayers?

2. What does it mean to you to realize that you have both Jesus and the Holy Spirit as your "advocates" before God the Father? How does this change the way you might pray for forgiveness for sin?

3. What is the most important or impacting lesson you've learned from this study of Mary? How can you apply those insights to your daily life?

PRACTICE

This week, go back over the previous sessions of this study. Note at least three things that were new to you or surprised you. Then pray the Hail, Holy Queen (found on page 160) and ask for Mary's intercession and guidance.

MARIAN PRAYERS

Hail Mary

Hail Mary, full of grace, the Lord is with thee. Blessed art thou among women, and blessed is the fruit of thy womb, Jesus.

Holy Mary, Mother of God, pray for us sinners, now and at the hour of our death. Amen.

The Angelus

V. The angel of the Lord declared unto Mary;
R. And she conceived by the Holy Spirit.
Hail Mary ...

V. Behold the handmaid of the Lord.
R. Be it done unto me according to your word.
Hail Mary ...

V. And the Word was made flesh,
R. And dwelt among us.
Hail Mary ...

V. Pray for us, O holy Mother of God,
R. That we may be made worthy of the promises of Christ.

Let us pray.
Pour forth, we beseech you, O Lord, your grace into our hearts, that we, to whom the incarnation of Christ, your Son, was made known by the message of an angel, may, by his passion and cross, be brought to the glory of his resurrection, through the same Christ our Lord.
R. Amen.

The *Memorare*

Remember, O most gracious Virgin Mary, that never was it known that anyone who fled to your protection, implored your help, or sought your intercession was left unaided.

Inspired by this confidence, I fly unto you, O virgin of virgins, my mother; to you do I come, before you I stand, sinful and sorrowful. O Mother of the Word Incarnate, despise not my petitions, but in your mercy hear and answer me. Amen.

The Litany of the Blessed Virgin Mary

Lord, have mercy on us.

Christ, have mercy on us.

Lord, have mercy on us.

Christ, hear us.

Christ, graciously hear us.

God the Father of heaven, — Have mercy on us.

God the Son, Redeemer of the world, — Have mercy on us.

God the Holy Spirit, — Have mercy on us.

Holy Trinity, one God, — Have mercy on us.

Holy Mary, — Pray for us.

Holy Mother of God, ...

Holy Virgin of virgins, ...

Mother of Christ, ...

Mother of the Church, ...

Mother of divine grace, ...

Mother most pure, ...

Mother most chaste, ...

Mother inviolate, ...

Mother undefiled, ...

Mother immaculate, ...

Mother most amiable, ...

Mother most admirable, ...

Mother of good counsel, ...

Mother of our Creator, ...

Mother of our Savior, ...

Virgin most prudent, ...   **Pray for us.**
Virgin most venerable, ...
Virgin most renowned, ...
Virgin most powerful, ...
Virgin most merciful, ...
Virgin most faithful, ...

Mirror of justice, ...
Seat of wisdom, ...
Cause of our joy, ...
Spiritual vessel, ...
Vessel of honor, ...
Singular vessel of devotion, ...
Mystical rose, ...
Tower of David, ...
Tower of ivory, ...
House of gold, ...
Ark of the covenant, ...
Gate of heaven, ...
Morning star, ...
Health of the sick, ...
Refuge of sinners, ...
Comforter of the afflicted, ...
Help of Christians, ...

Queen of angels, ...
Queen of patriarchs, ...
Queen of prophets, ...
Queen of apostles, ...
Queen of martyrs, ...
Queen of confessors, ...
Queen of virgins, ...
Queen of all saints, ...
Queen conceived without original sin, ...
Queen assumed into heaven, ...
Queen of the most holy Rosary, ...
Queen of peace, ...

V. Lamb of God, who takes away the sins of the world,

R. Spare us, O Lord.

V. Lamb of God, who takes away the sins of the world,

R. Graciously hear us, O Lord.

V. Lamb of God, who takes away the sins of the world,

R. Have mercy on us.

V. Pray for us, O holy Mother of God,

R. That we may be made worthy of the promises of Christ.

Let us pray.

O God, whose only-begotten Son, by his life, death, and resurrection, has purchased for us the rewards of everlasting life; grant, we beseech you, that we who meditate on these mysteries of the most holy Rosary of the Blessed Virgin Mary, may both imitate what they contain, and obtain what they promise. Through the same Christ our Lord. Amen.

Hail, Holy Queen

Hail, holy Queen, Mother of mercy. Hail, our life, our sweetness, and our hope. To you do we cry, poor banished children of Eve. To you do we send up our sighs, mourning and weeping in this valley of tears. Turn then, most gracious advocate, your eyes of mercy toward us, and after this, our exile, show unto us the blessed fruit of your womb, Jesus. O clement, O loving, O sweet Virgin Mary.